ONE MAN'S WAR

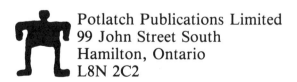

Potlatch Publications Limited
99 John Street South
Hamilton, Ontario
L8N 2C2

ONE MAN'S WAR

by
Stuart Waters

As well as I can remember, the incidents in *One Man's War*
are accurately described. In some instances I have forgotten
the names of those involved: in others I have, for my
own reasons, altered the names.

My thanks go to Robert Nielsen, president,
Potlatch Publications, for suggesting this book,
and to my wife Helen for the long hours she spent
typing the manuscript - and encouraging its author.

Cover illustration: Martin Springett
Maps: Michael Eddenden

ISBN 0-919676-27-8

Printed in Canada by
Johanns Graphics Ltd.,
Waterloo, Ontario

Dedicated to the memory of
Sergeant Alan Bellamy, Royal Artillery,
who was killed in action,
June 12, 1942.

CONTENTS

PART ONE

DARTFORD, 1939

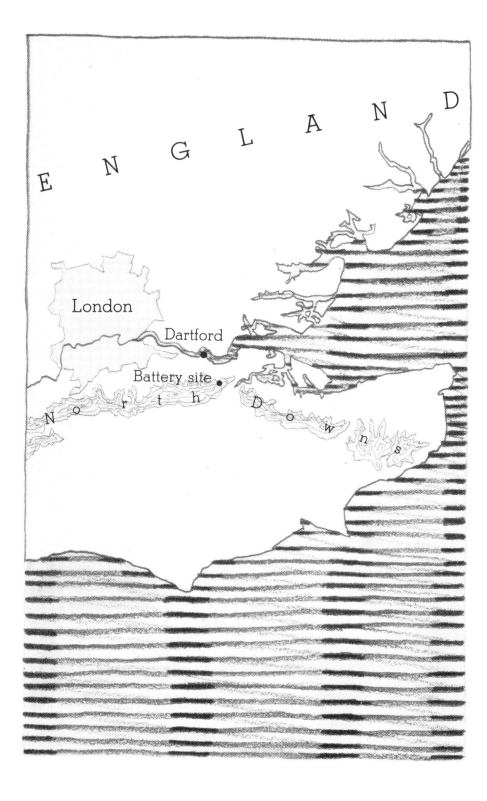

CHAPTER I

ADVANCE AND BE - RECOGNIZED?

There never was a good war or a bad peace.

Benjamin Franklin

This narrative begins when I put down my pen on the morning of September 1st, 1939, and walked out of the office where I worked. I hurried to the drill hall of the local Territorial Army infantry regiment, and offered my services. But did I not know there was a war on and service was for the duration? Why not wait to be conscripted? Besides, all the necessary documents were packed. I meekly said I understood their objections, but I was no raw recruit; I had already served five years as a "Saturday afternoon soldier" in the Artists' Rifles, and anyway, one volunteer was worth five pressed men. This was not well received, and I left them to their mugs of tea and cigarettes.

A few hundred yards farther on was the headquarters of the local anti-aircraft battery, Royal Artillery. Here I was welcomed, documented and told to return in the evening to be sworn in and taken to the gun-site. I was also advised to bring a pair of gumboots, overalls and the usual odds and ends necessary for an extended stay. So it was that I was sworn in as a soldier of the King, slept under canvas and paraded for breakfast.

That I had no uniform yet did not stop my being put on camp guard duty that night. The troop sergeant found some difficulty in mustering enough men for guard without including his friends. He regarded me as a godsend and I foresaw many such duties in future. Sergeant Parker found his responsibilities difficult, especially when they concerned writing, spelling and keeping lists. On one memorable occasion he rendered his guard and duties rota in such a state of confusion that he inadvertently put

11

himself down as guard commander. Too late he found out his mistake and the largest turnout of spectators ever known cheered the uninspiring guard-mounting ceremony and its accidental commander.

The guard tent was pitched behind the hedge which separated the gun-park from the road, and near the gate which gave access to the site. Each sentry on duty at the camp entrance served for two hours. He was then relieved for four hours before he stood guard again. The guard was mounted at six in the evening and dismissed at six next morning. Anyone who approached the gate was challenged by the sentry, throwing his bayoneted rifle to the on-guard position and calling, "Halt, who goes there?" If the answer was satisfactory, he would say, "Advance, friend, and be recognized." All being well, he would admit the man into the camp.

My first turn of duty ended at ten o'clock and I settled down to try to sleep until two a.m. Those who had left the camp for the evening began to return, many singing raucously. I had not yet gone to sleep when I heard the sentry challenge a singing gunner:

"Halt, who goes there?"

"Prick," came the coarse but not uncommon answer.

"Advance, Prick, and be circumcised," came the guard's instant reply.

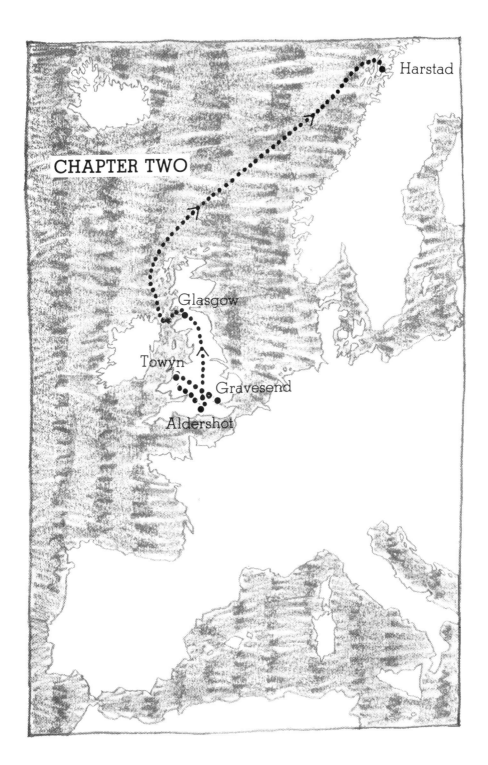

CHAPTER TWO

Harstad

Glasgow

Towyn

Gravesend

Aldershot

CHAPTER 2

IT'S WAR!
BUT DON'T BE UNKIND TO MUSSOLINI

War's a brain-spattering, windpipe-slitting art,
Unless her cause by right be sanctified.

Lord Byron

On enlisting, a recruit was asked to state his religious denomination. This was to ensure that, in the likely event in wartime of his burial, the Army could assign the appropriate chaplain to do the honours. Those without any particular conviction would usually choose Church of England ("C of E"). Nonconformists would indicate their particular sect, and Roman Catholics would staunchly own their faith. However, there were heretics. Some called themselves "R.C.s" believing that opportunity to attend Mass every Sunday was customary, which might cause them to miss some unpleasant duties. The "C. of E." heretics reasoned that the "R.C.s" would be back from church in time to do cook-house fatigues while their camp service was on.

Gunner Fuller had insisted on being recorded as a Sun Worshipper. This had required no little persistence to achieve. The arguments against were strongly put. Why couldn't he just be "C. of E.", "R.C.", or even Nonconformist? Everybody else was. Suppose he was killed in very hot weather, how long could they preserve him while they searched for an appropriate minister to bury him? Gunner Fuller said he didn't mind, just bury him.

On that first Sunday, Gunner Fuller was, predictably, cleaning the latrines. The Roman Catholics were peeling potatoes and the rest, fresh from their devotions, were enjoying a cigarette. Suddenly it was announced that the prime minister, Neville Chamberlain, would speak to the nation.

All who could gathered in the dining tent, where the wireless set was located. After his short address, the prime minister announced that, since no reply to Britain's ultimatum had been received from Germany, a state of war existed with that country. As he finished, the air-raid sirens wailed their warning. The camp alarm sounded and the guns were manned. The rest of us ran to our tents to pick up gas-masks, gas-capes and steel helmets, which we donned while struggling our way to the trenches. Airplanes could be heard approaching, and the bolder peeped over the parapets in case there was something to see, while others cowered. Three of our own planes flew low overhead, and as they did the "All Clear" sounded.

Those early days of September were busy. Gun-pits had to be sand-bagged; ammunition-pits, a first-aid post and long lengths of trenches dug. The trenches were to protect those not manning the guns during air-raids. We were expecting a deluge of bombs and poison gas from Germany. All over the camp pedestals were erected, bearing sheets of gas-sensitive card which would react to gases delivered in liquid form. There were no more warnings, but each day we worked for twenty minutes in gas-masks.

Within a few days the camp organization tightened, reducing chaos to mere disorder, and later to comparative orderliness. As a holder of a driver's licence I was detailed to drive and maintain the second-in-command's car. I had a perfunctory test performed by a junior officer reputed to be a reserve driver for the famous Auto-Union Team, the world's champions. He did most of the driving during the test, racing over blind crossroads at great speed while I visualised being hit broadside by a lorry. Lieutenant Clark had never heard of safe driving.

The car I was driving for the second-in-command had been hired, with many others, from a large distributor in London. As Army transport became available, the private cars were to be returned. A collection of these, with their drivers, were gathered at the regiment's headquarters near Gravesend. Our orders were to take the cars to the distributor's showrooms in Great Portland Street, London, and we made it a race. I had a definite advantage in knowing our exact destination and the quickest way there. This was the first car race I was ever in, and I won it.

No transport replaced these cars for a long time, so I became a Lewis gunner. The Lewis gun had been the main light machine-gun in World War One, both on land and in the air. In an anti-aircraft battery, its purpose was engaging low-flying planes. The 3-inch gun with which the Battery was equipped was also a

1914-18 veteran. In fact, on September 3rd, the Battery had only three such guns; a fourth was added in the first week of war, taken from the Imperial War Museum - literally a museum piece! Wielding our antique weapons, we drilled in the mounted drill of World War One - or even earlier. Unfortunately, however, we were on foot! The new Army battle dress uniforms were issued, but many old-timers still wore their breeches, long puttees and spurs. These accoutrements were not allowed on parade, but because of their sex appeal were considered ideal for evening leave with the local girls - though potentially dangerous until the sharp points of the rowels were filed down.

Wherever the Army gathers and beer is available, there is singing. The more famous Second World War songs had not yet been written, but we knew some from the previous war and other topical ditties. We were surprised when we were paraded and told that France and Britain were trying to keep Italy from following Germany into the war, or, at least, to remain neutral. It was therefore necessary for political reasons that we cease singing a song very popular with us, but derogatory to Signor Mussolini. The song had been current for some years but had not gained popular acceptance among the forces until recently. A few lines remain in my mind...

> Il Duce *gave the order to march against the foe*
> *And off to Abyssinia the organ-grinders go.*
> *Soon the organ-grinders have nothing left to grind;*
> *They're back to Mussolini with their organs left behind.*
>
> *The hosts of Ethiopia return to hearth and home*
> *With knick-knacks for the mantelpiece imported*
> *straight from Rome.*
> *The Pope is inundated with offers to join his choir*
> *From Mussolini's soldiers with voices an octave higher.*

This was sung to *John Brown's Body* and had a chorus of lewd suggestions of what might be done to Mussolini and Hitler.

Apart from training and drilling, we worked on improving the camp. A heavy rainstorm had made drainage trenches round the tents necessary, and there were always new ammunition-pits

16

to dig and the old ones to fill, in accordance with the Army belief that a busy soldier is a happy one. A chronic inability to site the ammunition-pit in the best position first time ensured very happy soldiers indeed.

One "Dig-a-new-and-fill-the-old" campaign came to an end with a radical change in our sanitary arrangements. These had consisted of a deep trench with a long pole for a seat, the whole rustic affair hidden by a canvas screen. Six brand new chemical toilets, from each of which rose a tall ventilation pipe, had been placed in a friendly circle, all facing inwards. The canvas screen now surrounded the companionable site.

Since our role was to defend a large factory making war supplies, the Lewis guns had to be placed nearer the target than the 3-inch guns so that attackers would be in range. We were moved to a low ridge, where we dug four gun-pits in the chalk of the North Downs. A new hut was built at the foot of the slope to house us and a telephone connected us with Battery Headquarters, which was near enough for our meals to be delivered, as we had no cooking facilities. We were nearer to the town than previously and enjoyed frequent evening leave.

November brought a change. The Battery moved to a firing camp in Towyn, situated on Cardigan Bay on the west coast of Wales. A long day's train journey ended about midnight and we marched to our billets, boarding houses on an esplanade only yards from the sea. All furniture had been removed and we were four or five to a room. A larger house was used for Battery office, kitchens and dining rooms. The day began with a march to the railway station after breakfast. A train took us to the park, some five miles away and right on the beach, where the guns and instruments were sited on a flat, well-grassed area. We experienced intensive gun-drill for several days, after which a target appeared, towed by a plane on the seaward side. The tow was some two thousand feet long because live ammunition was used. All shipping was prohibited in the area during the ensuing practice shoots.

The drills and shoots were closely observed by gunnery instructors, while a team of recorders kept details of the position of dials on gun, predictor and height-finder for each round fired. I was posted to the recorder detachment, which was made up from all the batteries at the camp. My first job was to keep the necessary data on a blackboard for the recorders to note the battery firing, the number of the practice series, and the number of that particular run of the target, or "sleeve" as it was called. Safety officers made certain the guns fired only within an arc which ensured the shells burst over the sea, and that the instruments were following the sleeve, not the plane towing it! In the excitement, the latter proved a most natural mistake - the plane was bigger, and represented precisely what we were being trained to shoot down - and if unchecked could result in a coolness on the part of the surviving pilots, if nothing worse.

The days were long but interesting. Sandwich lunches were eaten in a midday break and tea was made. Four o'clock was the usual time to end the practice and the train was waiting to take us back. A hot meal was served at five o'clock and, unless on duty, all were free until lights-out at ten-thirty. Towyn was well-provided to look after thirsty soldiers and there was a popular dance each Saturday night. For those who appreciated it, the hills and waterfalls of the countryside were a great attraction, and many of us spent Sundays walking. The weather through November into December remained mild, occasionally wet.

All the batteries were able to train on the 3.7-inch guns, which they hoped would replace the ancient and much less effective 3-inch variety. When the firing began on the bigger guns I had to leave my blackboard and chalk to note how near the pointers were to being coincident on the gun-layers' dial. The job of one gun-layer was to train the gun for elevation, the other for line. One pointer was activated electrically by the predictor and the other by the gun-layers, training the gun by hand. At the moment of firing, the pointers were to be exactly at the same point on the dial. The predictor was a computer, using as data the range of the target from the gun and the bearing of the target's direction of flight. The data were constantly changing and the accuracy of the prediction needed the two gun-layers to keep the target in the cross-wires of their telescopes, so that the predictor could determine the point in space where the target would be when a shell arrived.

The gun-layers and the recorders used small plugs of cotton-wool put loosely in their ears to prevent injury to eardrums, since both groups had their backs to the muzzle whence came the concussion and sound of the guns, the former like a kick in the pants, the latter a sharp pain in the eardrum. After making a note on one's report, there was always time to look at the target before the shell burst.

We had other diversions. One day the target-towing plane broke down and made a forced wheels-up landing on the beach in front of the guns, but without injury to the crew or much damage to the plane.

Most of us enjoyed the time at the camp. It was chilly in December, but our resident scrounger found a way through basements and cellars to the coal storage for the kitchen. As a result, each evening until lights-out we enjoyed a fire, which we banked up as far as the small grate would allow. We had to stand by our beds one morning towards the end of our stay while the rooms were inspected and a sharp-eyed officer noticed one of the bars of the grate in our room was broken.

"How did that happen?" he asked the room in general. I answered him, misleadingly but truthfully.

"Sir, I think it snapped one bitterly cold night." And so it had, but it was red-hot when it broke!

All of us were given seven days leave for Christmas, and the recorders, as a reward for their good work, were to report back to the firing camp, although their batteries had finished there. This meant we would continue as a unit on our own, without the usual regimental duties to perform. I was pleased with this decision. Furthermore, in the hope of a Christmas leave, I had obtained a special licence. My fiancee came to Towyn and we were married in the presence of all the recorders, who then marched us up the high street to drink the health of the bride and bridegroom.

Training continued in the firing camp after Christmas and the recording job went on until the end of January. We were then returned to our units. Only a week after my return, volunteers were sought to join a battery under orders for overseas service, and as I felt unsettled and bored, I applied.

Our new unit was equipped with 3.7-inch guns and I joined it at a gun-site protecting Hornchurch Aerodrome, in Essex near the Thames Estuary. Here I became a telephonist in a command post where the telephone was connected to the Operations Control Headquarters. As this was still during the so-called "Phoney

War" - the uncertain period between the German invasion of Poland and their advance into Scandinavia - no air-raid warnings were received, but we were constantly given exercises, especially in the small hours of the night shift. These consisted of a succession of messages giving the number of enemy aircraft, their position as a grid-map reference and their height. We took down the information, were asked later to read it back, and corrections were made. The dugout was heated with an oil stove and a hot drink could be made to help while away the night hours.

Ammunition-pits still needed to be dug, and equipped with ammunition. Moving 3.7-inch shells, which weighed sixty pounds, was a test of strength and endurance, especially when they came in boxes of two! To transport the ammunition from one place to another a human chain was formed, each man having one end of a box in each hand, the end man being the luckiest. I felt torn apart by the boxes and wondered how I could keep going. It happened that the sergeant in charge of the move, who was not very popular, chose to upbraid us for being slow. At this Bombardier Carter put down his load and everyone followed his example. Carter said he would prove he was not slow, and challenged the sergeant to do as he would; carry two full boxes on his own. The sergeant not unnaturally refused, but Carter pointed to two boxes and bet the sergeant a pound he could carry them to the new ammunition-pit. The bet was on. With a great effort Carter lifted one box on his shoulder and the other under his arm. The sergeant, seeing the strain Carter was under, begged him to put them down, and even said the bet was off. Carter said he would do it, but it was obvious it was too much for him; his legs were buckling as he staggered. The sergeant, very worried now, implored him to put the boxes down. Suddenly Carter gasped, "Catch them, Sarge, I can't do it!"

The sergeant held out his arms, braced for the great weight, and Carter managed to drop the boxes on them. The two boxes rose about ten feet in the air before falling, and by then Carter was lying on the ground in a paroxysm of laughter, in which we all joined. The boxes were empty! Henceforth we took our time with the carrying, the sergeant having left us to recover some of his dignity.

We moved to a local village hall close to the Army Medical Post, where we received typhoid and tetanus inoculations, after which we were allowed leave for the rest of the day. It was a one-room hall with no separate room for the sergeants, and while we were all in bed by 10:30 when the senior bombardier turned the lights out, the sergeants came in noisily about 11:30 and turned them back on. This was too much for Gordon Deck. He rose out of his blankets, some six feet four inches of him towering angrily above us.

"Either we have some rules here, or we haven't a single bloody rule and we all do what we like."

With his speech finished, he picked up a chair and threw it up to the rafters. It fell with a splintering crash and there was silence. Someone turned out the lights and the late comers bedded down quietly.

It had been generally thought that the unit was destined for Finland, but as the days of March were torn off the calendar, an intervention in that country seemed unlikely to succeed, or - if it did - be in time. When we finally moved to Aldershot to be equipped, we felt sure that Finland would not be our destination. We would know soon enough, when handed either tropical or arctic clothing.

Guns, gun-tractors, trucks of all sorts and motorcycles were the first of our new equipment to reach us. A shortage of dispatch riders gave me a change of occupation and I took over a heavy B.S.A. motorcycle which I rode round and round until I felt safe. Before we knew whither we were bound, orders for our move were given. The first day's march was to Catterick, an army base in Yorkshire.

There were many delays and difficulties during that first day. The dispatch riders acted like sheepdogs, herding the convoy along, reporting to the Light Aid Detachment in their breakdown truck any vehicles in difficulty, waiting at crossroads, T-junctions or forks to point out routes, rounding up those who had made wrong turns and others who had followed them. Soon after midday the N.C.O. in charge of us took my bike, as his own had broken down. I rode with a friend in a small car which was carrying our equipment and kit-bags. The long day finally ended, and we reached Catterick to be given tepid stew and rice pudding before bedding down on a concrete floor in an unswept barrack block.

After an equally unpalatable breakfast, our way led over the hills of the Lake District to Carlisle and on to Dumfries for the night. Our reception at Dumfries was very different from that at Catterick. A good meal and clean sleeping quarters were provided, though there were no bath or shower facilities. I went to a large hotel nearby and asked if I could have a bath. The clerk said many Army officers were billeted there but he would see what he could do. An officer of the Royal Scots was standing near and overheard the conversation. He told the clerk that I could have his room and would he see that there were plenty of towels. I shaved and bathed in comfort.

I found my friends in a pub and tried to buy a drink. The locals refused to allow it. They insisted on ordering a "hauf and hauf" for all of us, and another and another. Some of us were a little bleary-eyed next morning as we drove through the valleys and over the hills towards Glasgow and, finally, to Greenock, where we were housed in a warehouse converted to temporary barracks. Our guns and vehicles were parked on the docks just below our windows.

The loading of our guns, gun-tractors, all other vehicles and heavy equipment was held up next morning because the stevedores went on strike. By now we had definite news - our destination was Norway. This gave us a sense of urgency, and Sergeant Scanes, who had Navy experience, was ready to take over the loading, if the strike was not settled, with a hand-picked gang. The rest of us were free for the day.

We continued to enjoy Scottish hospitality. In restaurants, prices were drastically cut to meet our two-shillings-a-day wages. We were also near enough to experience the famous "Saturday night in Glasgow." As we came out of a very friendly pub in Greenock at closing time into the blackout, an extraordinary scene became visible as our eyes grew accustomed to the darkness. There were bodies in shop entrances, on the pavement, in the gutter, held up by lampposts and those trying to avoid, with exaggerated care, their fallen comrades.

All good things come to an end. Our equipment was now loaded in the cargo ship and we boarded the S.S. *Empress of Australia,* which had not yet been converted to a troop ship. We occupied cabins and were served meals by stewards. The weather was kind though cold as we sailed north, and a destroyer escort gave us a sense of security. On the second day, one of the destroyers suddenly "bleeped" several times and stopped right ahead of us. We steered away to avoid her and saw the reason for the hubbub; a mine was floating loose and the escort had spotted it and warned us. We passed quite close and shortly afterwards heard the rifle fire by which the mine would be holed and sunk.

On the fourth day we sighted land, snow covered and barren. We entered a fiord some hours later and found ourselves without our escort. As the fiord narrowed, room for manoeuvring became less, ideal for the enemy to bomb. Almost as if the pilot had read our thoughts, a Heinkel bomber found us. The alarm sounded and everyone went below. Gunner Roberts, who had a camera, and I lingered to be last off the deck. The plane came low and dropped a single bomb which landed about one hundred yards from the ship. Roberts snapped the explosion but both of us were surprised and frightened by the fierce crackling sound, not the dull boom we had expected.

We anchored in the endless twilight of the Arctic summer nights and were taken off by trawlers converted by the Royal Navy to mine-sweepers, mine-layers, patrol-ships, and maids of all work. They were from the fishing fleets of ports along the English and Scottish east coast. They took us to Harstad, a small port on the island of Hinnoy, the largest of the Vesteralen Islands. Here we gathered on the docks while the rest of the Battery arrived. I saw two small Norwegian boats delivering casualties from the land fighting near Narvik, which was still held by the Germans. They were French Alpine troops, the famous *Chasseurs-Alpins,* and many were suffering from frostbite, a reminder that we were well inside the Arctic Circle, even if it was the month of May.

Shortly after midnight we marched off to a small church on the outskirts of Harstad. We had carried our bedding and packs with us so that we were able to sleep till morning.

Harstad, though small, was the Navy and Army base for the campaign to take Narvik, destroy it, and thereby deny its use as a German port for the iron from the mines at Gaellevare in Sweden. The port for this purpose in the Baltic was Lulea, ice-bound for half the year, in contrast to Narvik, which was free of ice, year-round, and connected by rail to the Swedish mines.

23

There were also an oil refinery and storage tanks in Harstad. The Germans were bombing it regularly so that anti-aircraft guns were urgently needed until a landing-ground was ready at Bardufoss, about twenty miles farther north.

PART TWO

NARVIK, 1941

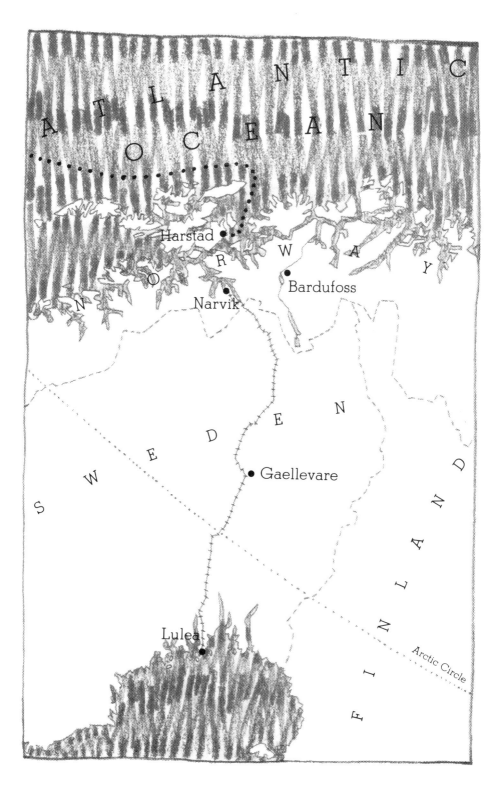

CHAPTER 3

ARCTIC CAMPAIGN

*The enemy is anybody who's going to get you killed
no matter which side he's on.*

Joseph Heller

The cargo ship with our heavy equipment arrived in Harstad the next day and unloaded. Reinstated as dispatch rider, I went to the dock to collect my motorcycle. While I was there, Harstad was bombed. Much of the bombing was directed against the cruiser H.M.S. *Effingham,* but she escaped damage.

The gun-site where I was located had but two guns, and was on high ground about three miles south of Harstad. After being shown the site, I went back to lead the guns to it. This was soon done, and with some show of self-importance as I herded a small convoy of French troops to one side, telling them, with restrained conceit for my accent, *"Les grands canons D.C.A. approchent."*

This produced so much rapid French in reply that my *"ouis"* and *"nons"* may have been somewhat random.

Our living quarters at the site were in a derelict cowshed. While the guns were being brought into action, the rest of us started cleaning and repairing our new home. The ground was frozen and we were able to shovel off a top layer to give a clean foundation. The stalls were intact and, instead of one cow, now housed two men. The chinks were filled and loose boards secured. We had been promised a stove, but it seemed that in preparing the expedition no one realized how cold it is inside the Arctic Circle even in May. Another instance of faulty planning was the lack of sunglasses in a land of heavy snow and dazzling sunshine. The glare was painful, even to the point of snow-blindness for some.

My duties included a daily trip to Battery Headquarters with a report on men, equipment and ammunition. This was usually given to me about 6 p.m. On the third day in the new site the weather was exceptionally cold and, while returning from headquarters, my face became numb. I stopped at the Medical Aid Post. Three medical orderlies whom I had met on the *Empress* rubbed my face until it painfully regained full feeling. I had been near frostbite. The gun-site commander did not seem to believe the explanation for my late return.

Next day, as I rode into Harstad on my way to headquarters, a very fierce air-raid began, aimed at the oil storage tanks. By the time I reached the hill which led down to the town, several houses were in flames and some people were struggling out of one of them carrying a man in a zinc bath. He had been wounded, and I learned there were other casualties when I stopped to see if help was needed. They begged me to arrange for an ambulance. The military hospital was on the road to headquarters and, as everybody had gone to ground, I had the road to myself and drove as fast as I could. When I reached the hospital, I turned into the driveway at a great clip and rode headlong into a brick wall. Instead of bouncing back on impact, the bike climbed the wall and I fell over backwards, luckily letting go and avoiding the bike. I stopped the engine, retrieved my helmet, and went into the hospital. The Matron was standing in the hall, coolly directing the patients down to the basement.

"We'll do what we can," she said, when I told her that civilian casualties on the hill near the tanks needed an ambulance. As I picked up my bike, a 15 cwt. truck came in with wounded Coldstream Guards.

It had long been realized that fighter aircraft were necessary to protect the Army - then attacking Narvik, but under constant heavy bombing - and also to cover oil tanks, dock installations and naval craft under repair in Harstad harbour. Two landing strips were being constructed, one at Skaanland, a few miles east of Harstad, and another at Bardufoss, about twenty miles north of Narvik. The former was in marshy ground and had to be abandoned, but the latter was now ready, and we were to go there to give anti-aircraft defence.

The guns, gun-tractors and other vehicles went back to the docks, since our journey had to be made by boat to reach the mainland. I took my motorcycle down to be loaded. Nearby was the destroyer *Eskimo,* whose bows had been very badly damaged by a torpedo in the second Battle of Narvik. *Eskimo* had had to steam stern foremost to reach Harstad afloat. Our heavy equipment left and we followed next day.

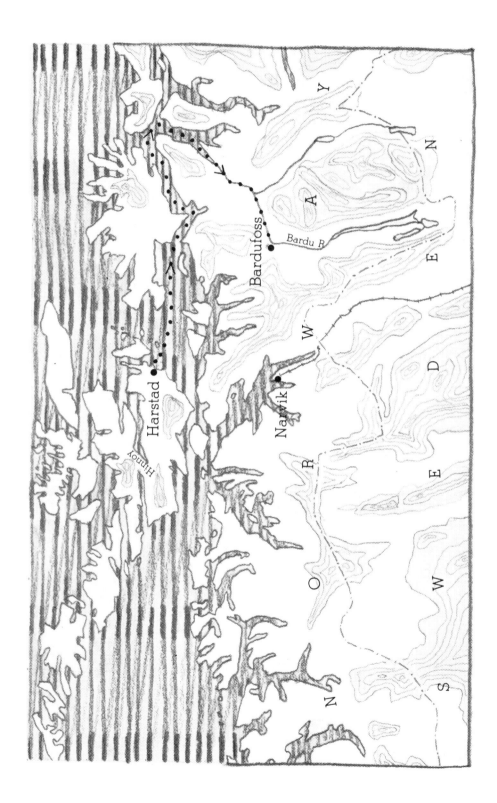

CHAPTER 4

A NORWEGIAN "THREE-HOLER"

War is delightful to those who have no experience of it.
Erasmus

Our voyage from Harstad up the fiord was interesting. We travelled aboard the Norwegian fishing boats that were powered by a large single-cylinder diesel engine. We named them by the distinctive noise the engines made. "Chug-chug."

We landed at a small village and the gun-tractors were waiting for us. The snow was melting and the unpaved roads were deep in mud. Even with four-wheel drive, the powerful trucks were hard put to keep going. Suddenly a soldier was seen standing in the middle of the road, apparently on top of the mud. He waved his arms, but did not move out of our path. We stopped inches from him. No, he couldn't move because he'd sink right into the mud. Well, how could he stand there where he was without sinking into it?

"I'm a dispatch rider," he said, "and I'm standing on my bike."

We took him aboard and, a few miles farther on, turned off the road into a field, part of a small farm. There was a large barn, three storeys of wooden construction on a stone foundation. A long ramp led up to the first wooden floor, which was occupied by cattle. Fifty yards away, to one side of the barn, stood a farmhouse.

Nearby was the new R.A.F. airfield, and some Gloucester Gladiators, fighters of the early thirties, were stationed there. These would soon be replaced by nine Hurricanes flown in from an aircraft carrier. Both airfield and village were named Bardufoss, after the River Bardu which ran close to the farm.

For the first few days we slept out in the open, around our guns. We were very cosy in our sleeping bags but it was hard to leave them in the cold mornings. Already near the end of May the sun was visible for twenty hours, and it was never dark. Before we left, the sun merely dipped to the horizon and then began the long slow ascent of the sky. We were well inside the Arctic Circle, about 70° N. latitude.

We were given the freedom of a room in the barn, on the same level as the cattle stalls, as a lavatory. It was on the farmhouse side of the barn, and was reached by a short flight of steps. The door had a simple latch, but no lock or other means of securing it. Along one wall was a long box bench in which three holes, each covered with a lid, had been cut. Gunner Fanshawe, a strong, dependable soldier, was the first visitor to enjoy the use of this convenience. He returned, after a very short stay, pale and shaken, hardly coherent. No sooner had he dropped his trousers and sat down on the middle hole, he told us, than two of the farmhouse servants entered, hoisted their skirts, and joined him, one on each side.

"Scared me shitless," he reported, whether literally or metaphorically he never did explain.

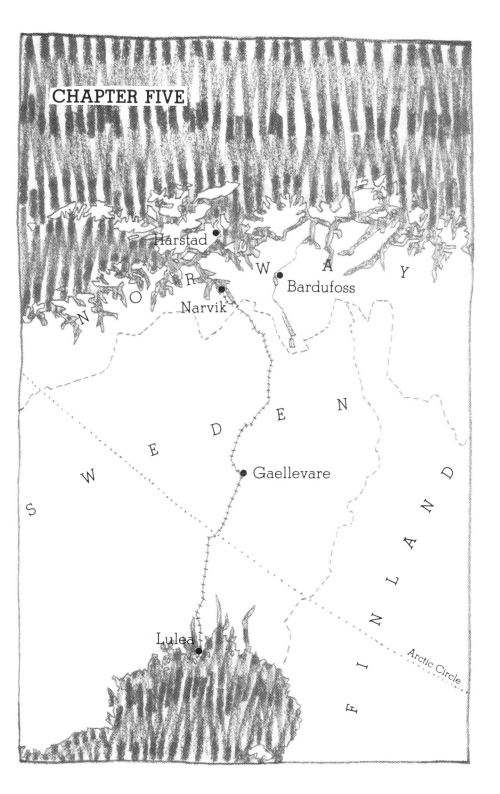

CHAPTER 5

A LET-DOWN ON THE PLAYING FIELDS OF ETON...

The Battle of Waterloo was won on the playing fields of Eton.
attributed to the Duke of Wellington

We settled down quickly in our new home. The top attic-like floor of the barn became our sleeping quarters, once the farmer was convinced we were to be trusted and the Germans were not very active.

At Bardufoss we had a unique reveille. Neither bugle, nor trumpet, nor officious sergeant roused us each morning. Our reveille was silent. The cattle were still penned inside the barn and had been for the entire winter. At six o'clock precisely each morning the cowman mucked out their byre. Trapdoors were opened in each stall and the droppings were shovelled down to the midden below. All of us awakened instantly, even the heaviest sleeper. Down the ladder from our attic and down the stairs to the ramp and down that to the sweet open air we tumbled to escape the steaming stench.

The war was still being waged even though we enjoyed a respite. Narvik was in Allied hands and the German effort was restricted to an occasional high level reconnaissance flight. One very misty morning we heard aircraft - not Hurricanes, our experienced ears told us. We raced to the guns but before we reached them three Heinkel seaplanes roared over us one hundred feet up.

"Action, enemy planes!" was shouted from the command post, but almost at once we saw Norwegian Air Force markings. Nobody had thought to mention that our Allies had some German aircraft.

We had been able, during the lull, to do the necessary digging, wash our clothes in hot water, write letters, and generally organize our life. Road repairs had become our daily occupation, as our heavy vehicles had made huge ruts. On one such task we worked near a small shop, where I bought some brown crumbly goat's-milk cheese. Jimmy Rowan wanted to buy some booze, but after a conversation of signs and pidgen Norwegian, concluded that none existed in this part. Nevertheless, he came out of the shop with a bottle. What was in it was drinkable, though certainly not alcoholic.

Much of our talk concerned the possibility of a long stay here if the High Command wanted to keep a second foothold in Europe. We had arrived in Norway early enough to know how severe the long winter could be. We were not anxious to experience it. Already rumour or wishful thinking had it that we were to be relieved by Canadian troops, much more accustomed to the rigours of Arctic cold.

Meanwhile, near the end of May, the dusk of the small hours was lighter. The farm people seemed to sleep very little. Apparently they made up for it in December, when it was dark all day. The cattle had been let out of the barn, very shaky in the legs after their long confinement as they tottered out to graze.

Someone had acquired a wireless and we all listened each evening to the B.B.C. news bulletins. The steadily worsening reports had dispelled early optimism. One evening, news of the surrender of King Leopold of the Belgians reached us. Bombardier Yuell, who sported an upturned moustache of the kind affected by some R.A.F. pilots, and had a habit of stroking it upward while delivering his opinions, took violent exception to the news of the Belgian Army's capitulation at the King's orders.

"I just don't believe it. Don't you see, the Germans are cutting in on the B.B.C. broadcasts with lies and propaganda. I can't believe it. It's impossible for a man of King Leopold's calibre to surrender. Why, the man was at Eton!"

"Think Heaven Churchill was at Harrow," someone said softly.

PART THREE

GIBRALTAR, 1941

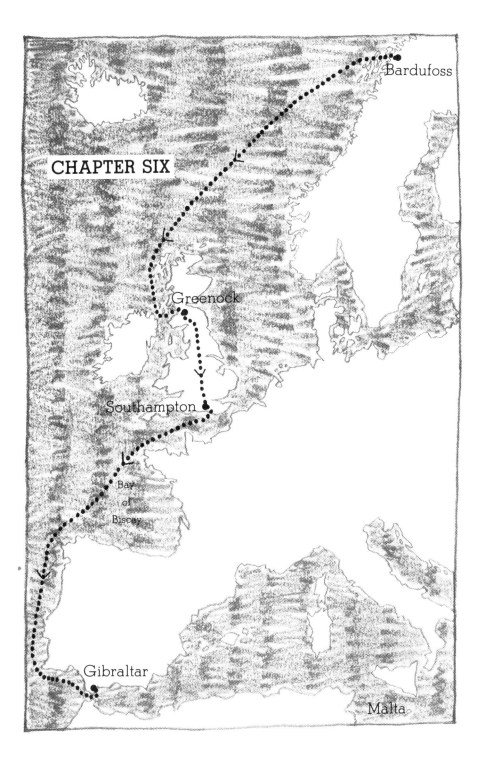

Bardufoss

Greenock

Southampton

Bay
of
Biscay

Gibraltar

Malta

CHAPTER 6
EVACUATION - AND AWAY AGAIN

They shall have wars and pay for their presumption.

Shakespeare

We had news of the beginning of the Dunkirk evacuation before our own. On June 6th we destroyed our guns, and the gun-tractors took us down to the small port on the fiord where we had landed. We rested in the pine woods near the landing stage till the morning of the next day. We boarded the small Norwegian fishing boats - the "Chug-chugs" - again and headed out into the fiord. It was a very misty morning, suitable for a retreat. About two hours later, a destroyer raced up and we climbed up the nets. Our boat was near the bows of the destroyer and we were burdened with all our kit, which made the ascent very difficult.

Climbing up a net is very different from running up a ladder. The net is not stable and swings disconcertingly. After the first few upward steps, the overhang began to affect me. I felt I would fall backwards and the bulky and heavy pack suddenly seemed four times heavier. It was only with an exhausting effort that I finally reached an outstretched hand and was hauled aboard.

The transfer was accomplished with all dispatch and the Navy made gallons of their own life-giving brand of cocoa for us. This I sipped gratefully, watching the immense bow-wave the destroyer made. We were soon out of sight of land and making for a convoy of troopships with escorts which circled as they awaited us. We were put aboard the *Monarch of Bermuda,* a luxury cruise ship in peacetime.

We were a motley collection. There were French Foreign Legion, *Chasseurs-Alpins,* and British troops of many units, though our own battery was the most numerous. I practised my French on the *Chasseurs,* all of whom on the ship were priests from a large monastery. One of the legionnaires had a German's head in his kit-bag, which called for a constant queue of admiring onlookers at the cabin door.

I found a friend on board, one of the crew, and I enjoyed his hospitality each evening in his cabin. When I had fallen off the motorcycle at the hospital, I had grazed my hand. It had become infected and would not respond to treatment. Long hours of sleep and good food did the trick and before we reached Scotland it had healed.

Our voyage was uneventful, save for one fleeting view of a German bomber. The Battery had mustered on the afterdeck, the only time we did so during the trip, when a Dornier 17 - the "Flying Pencil" - flew out of a low cloud immediately overhead. The pilot must have been as surprised as we were for it took him a few seconds to realize what was below him, and he dropped a stick of bombs which straddled the M.V. *Batory,* a Polish ship, but did no damage.

The escort left us and on the evening of the fourth day we sailed up the Clyde to Greenock where we disembarked. We were taken to a tented camp near Troon. There was a sandy beach only a few yards away and a pay parade was a great help to enjoying an evening out. Half the Battery went on a three-day leave and the less fortunate of us had an easy time waiting for our turn. The leave party returned, but by then the Battery had been warned for immediate overseas service and no more leave could be granted. This caused some bitterness because those of us left behind had done nothing useful while the others were on leave and could see no reason why we couldn't have gone with them. Furthermore, all of those who in February had volunteered to join the Battery seemed to be among the unfortunates who were not granted leave. How had the choice been made to decide who should go on the first leave party?

Our grievances were submerged as we entrained, with no knowledge - only speculation - of our destination. The train took us down the L.M.S. tracks through Carlisle, Preston, Crewe, Rugby, and then branched off to Basingstoke, thence straight through to Southampton. I looked out the window as we slowed down and saw a huge board which said, simply, "Dock Yards" below an arrow. The train pulled up, after passing through the dock gates, only some forty yards from a ship, the *City of Cairo*. The area round the ship and train was cordoned off by "Red-caps", the Military Police. While we waited to embark, I wrote a hurried note to my wife, which I entrusted to one of the Military Police.

We soon learned from the ship's crew that we were going to Gibraltar. Apart from the fact that I had never been there, I could think of no good reason for going. The *City of Cairo* was ill-prepared for the voyage: there were far more passengers than there were bunks in the hold, and the sanitary facilities were inadequate - a row of twelve doorless cubicles, each with a wooden seat and a bucket, had been secured on deck. I did not obtain a berth and slept on a narrow bench in the after dining room.

There was no naval escort for this ship. Some Lewis guns were placed on the bridge, on the afterdeck, and at the prow. It was to the last named that I was directed for a two-hour stint as we crossed the Bay of Biscay. It was not rough, but the swell was about forty feet. At the top I clung to the post on which the gun was mounted, to prevent myself from sliding down the deck. As the ship dropped into the trough between the crests, I hung on desperately to prevent myself from sliding overboard, and at all times I tried to vomit neatly to leeward to avoid fouling the deck. The normal complement for a Lewis gun is two, and several drums of ammunition should be available. So with a single drum of ammunition and no spares, with a very unstable gun-platform and a lone seasick marksman, the forward anti-aircraft defences of the *City of Cairo* posed little problem to a determined attacker.

At that time, towards the end of June 1940, the Allies still controlled the Atlantic coast of Europe. We had a safe voyage to Gibraltar which we reached in very hot weather on June 21st, just two weeks after leaving Norway well north of the Arctic Circle.

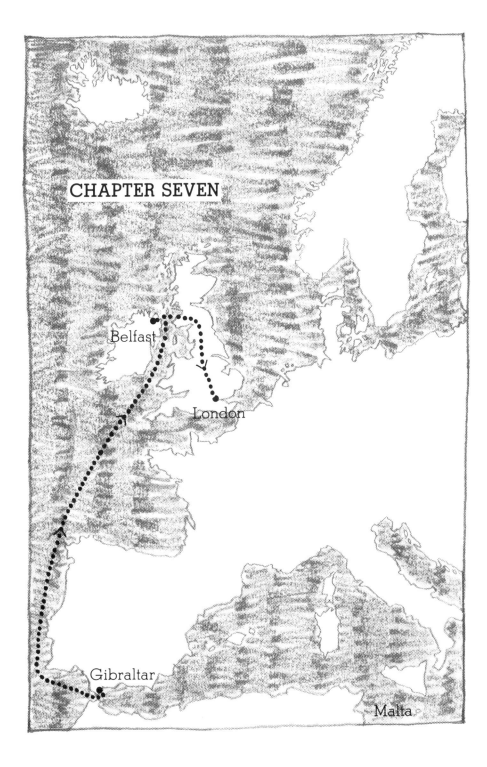

CHAPTER SEVEN

Belfast

London

Gibraltar

Malta

CHAPTER 7
ON THE ROCK - AND HOME

Gibraltar has been a British possession since 1704.
Whitaker's Almanac

It was a short march from the ship to our barracks, but a very uncomfortable one. We were wearing the same clothes we had worn in Norway. On a hot afternoon in late June, long johns and battledress are not suitable dress in Gibraltar!

Our quarters were newly built, two-storey buildings with small rooms, sleeping three at most. A large one-floor building had kitchens, dining room, bathrooms and showers. Nearby was the N.A.A.F.I. canteen. Beer flowed, billiard balls clicked and "housey-housey" numbers could be heard for miles over a public address system.

The setting reeked of The Rock's history. In one corner was a small dock, which in Nelson's time was used for refittings of the "wooden walls" of England. Just above the site was King's Bastion, part of the defences built in the early days of British occupation. From the Bastion it was a very short walk to Gibraltar's main street, where wine and beer flowed, castanets clacked and fists thudded on flesh as the Army and Navy kept up the traditional brawls. This, of course, was the peacetime sport of the Forces, for the war had not yet brought an armistice to their hostilities.

We soon learned all there was to know about The Rock. The Barbary apes were fed by the Army to make sure they stayed, since, according to tradition, Britain would lose Gibraltar when the last ape left. When the low clouds shrouded the top of the rock, the apes would come down from their high quarters to the town, swinging acrobatically from roof to roof. We quickly learned that Gibraltar depended on rainfall for fresh water. The sides of the rock were catchments leading the run-off into reservoirs. Our showers and baths were taken in salt water, with salt-water soap. In peacetime there had been a ferry service to Algeciras and Tangiers, but these were now cut off, and since Gibraltar was only two and three-quarter miles long and one mile wide, the effect was almost claustrophobic. This affected me, as dispatch riders were reduced to two in Battery Headquarters. Jimmy Rowan and I were no longer needed. Jim joined a gun detachment and I became a Lewis gunner again.

Italy, when it was obvious that France was defeated, had declared war on the Allies. Since Gibraltar was within range of bombers flying from Sardinia, it was the first target. At that time Gibraltar's air defences had no radar and the Italian bombers were able to attack without much risk. Little damage and very few casualties resulted. Our arrival greatly increased and improved the anti-aircraft defences and only a few ineffective raids were attempted. Malta was a much easier target for the Italians.

By the beginning of July we had settled down, our guns emplaced below the King's Bastion on what had been a football pitch. The French fleet had left its home ports and was in Oran, showing no disposition to join de Gaulle's Free French movement. If this fleet were to fall under German or Italian control, the British position in the Mediterranean would be hopeless. The French admiral at Oran would not join de Gaulle; neither would he join Britain, nor agree to scuttle or dismantle the fleet. The threat was too great for any more diplomatic efforts; Churchill sent a direct order to Admiral Somerville to destroy the French fleet. This most unpleasant task was carried out. As a reprisal, the French bombed Gibraltar for two days. One hundred and fifty bombers were used on the first day and our guns were constantly in action. Gunner Cooper and I had a good view from our Lewis gun pit, but no targets, as the planes bombed from about twenty thousand feet. However, we did feel some measure of participation when a bomb fell about twenty yards away and rained rocks and gravel on us. Next day one lone bomber dived and flew low across the dockyards, enabling us to empty a drum of ammunition at it, while about fifty others bombed from a safe height.

The French attack did more damage than the Italian; after emergency repairs to the water and gas mains in our kitchens, there was gas coming out of the taps and water out of the burners! The attacks were not repeated but some of the French pilots stole their planes to fly to Gibraltar, risking the very short emergency landing-strip in order to join the Free French.

Hitler and Franco met. The dictators were both seeking advantages from the events that had followed the fighting in Europe. The possibilities arising from a rapport between these men had caused much activity in Gibraltar. A company of hard-rock engineers from the Canadian Army had arrived to blast tunnels in the rock for gun emplacements, facing Spain. All Army units had to supply work parties to dig out the debris after the blasting. We did not enjoy this. Everybody had to do an eight-hour shift once a week. A very narrow gauge rail was laid in the tunnel right up to the rock face. After the explosions we pushed a truck up to the debris, shovelled it full of rubble, and then pushed it back. When all the pieces were cleared, the engineers came in to blast again. Six or eight charges would be placed and arranged to detonate one at a time; the explosions were counted to make sure all charges had worked.

Unfortunately this did not always happen. One day, while shovelling, I turned up an undetonated stick of gelignite, luckily without disaster. Some of the Black Watch were not so lucky. Apparently a shovel struck a stick causing it to explode, and there were fatalities. On the following Sunday, the chaplain conducting our service claimed that, despite the sadness, theirs had been a sacrifice for the country just as surely as death at the hands of the enemy. Some of the Battery took exception to this; they believed that some comments on safety precautions - or lack of them - would have been more useful as an epitaph than *Dulce et decorum est pro patria mori.*

Gibraltar had an important job ensuring that cargoes destined for Germany or German-occupied countries did not reach their destinations. Any ships that attempted to escape the blockade were arrested, brought into Gibraltar and the cargoes confiscated. As a result, we had our share of a cargo of eggs that was given to the Forces and later there were large bunches of green bananas ripening in our quarters.

The air-raids by the Italians and French had demonstrated that our barracks were too far away from the guns, and we were

44

moved into Nissen huts much closer to the gun-park. We had managed to establish our own canteen in one of the huts, and with the profits we hoped to add some extras to our rations which, though nourishing, lacked variety. A small committee, of which I was one, handled this and while I was in town I spent the money on swordfish, a much approved choice.

I was dissatisfied with the Lewis gun. To obtain a change of occupation, I quietly studied the duties of the gun-position officer's assistant, the "G.P.O. Ack." Control of the guns at all times is the responsibility of an officer, and his assistant is always a non-commissioned officer. I had heard that the G.P.O. Acks doing the job were not satisfactory. The duties, when in action, were onerous. The instruments - the predictor and the height-finder - were put on to the target after the spotter's telescope had found it. Then the G.P.O. Ack. would call the angle of sight and bearing of the target to the instruments. The officer would decide if the target was hostile, and, if it was, when to fire. All his orders were relayed by the G.P.O. Ack.

In due time I felt competent, and requested an opportunity to become a G.P.O. Ack. This was granted, and for a time I enjoyed the prestige and the interest of the position. All went well until some exercises were held, with observer-officers present to judge the efficiency of the site. In their report it was noted that I was a gunner; in the event of the officer becoming a casualty, it was not permissible for a mere gunner to take command. However, this did not occur until shortly before I left Gibraltar, and so my return to the Lewis gun was for a few weeks only.

I walked down to the water's edge after breakfast on a fine sunny day, feeling somewhat pensive. The outlook for all of us on Gibraltar was spending the rest of the war there without firing another shot in anger. This was not a pleasing future in such cramped surroundings and limited facilities. Whilst I was thus ruminating, there was a tremendous explosion, and a vast column of water rose just off the end of one of the moles in the harbour. About one hundred yards from this upheaval was the battleship H.M.S. *Barham,* moored alongside the mole. We heard that the explosion was caused by a torpedo ridden into the vicinity of the harbour by two Italian sailors. They fired it at the battleship, but it detonated on the boom protecting the harbour. The sailors were picked up.

My father died unexpectedly in January 1941 and I requested a return to the United Kingdom. There were many such requests, but, because of the extreme shortage of shipping, few were granted. However, my wife had made an appeal to our Member of Parliament, and I was surprised when I was informed I was on two hours' notice to take passage to England. A friend in Battery Headquarters told me that my original request had gone straight into the wastepaper basket! The day after I had been put on standby, a truck took me to the aircraft carrier *Furious*. I joined about fifty other "Army personnel taking passage", as we were called on board. There were very few planes on the *Furious;* she was returning from Malta, where she had delivered a load of fighters. We were housed in one of the hangars equipped with comfortable camp-cots.

The convoy slipped out of Gibraltar in darkness and turned east as though to go back to Malta. Next morning our direction was northwest, and we were joined by the aircraft carrier *Ark Royal,* the battle cruiser *Renown,* the cruiser *Sheffield* and six destroyers. Later that day we accompanied a large liner with its naval escort, taking home the Forces' families and other civilians from Hong Kong. During the night, the capital ships left to return to Gibraltar, leaving us with a destroyer escort.

One of the Army officers taking passage approached me on the second day and asked if I had seen a Canadian soldier who had managed to board the carrier at Gibraltar without authorisation and was now in hiding. I knew nothing and said so, but this encouraged me to ask others about the man. The Canadian came to meals in our mess and I saw him on one occasion. He was a tall, raw-boned man with red hair. His story was simple. He had been stationed in Glasgow before coming to Gibraltar. There he had become engaged to a girl and subsequent recent correspondence had indicated his return was required to marry his intended before a rapidly approaching deadline. He had heard of *Furious's* readiness to return home, and, while on an evening off duty, had managed to slip on board unnoticed. Undoubtedly some members of the crew were helping him.

All of us Army personnel were given "Action Stations" and "Abandon Ship Stations." On the fifth day out of Gibraltar the alarm rang for "Action Stations." The Captain announced over the Tannoy system that word had been received that three four-engined long-range enemy bombers were heading towards the convoy, and that sinking the *Furious* would be their objective. The Skuas, the Fleet Air fighters on board, flew off to meet them. The "Stand-down" was ordered after some twenty minutes. Later we heard that the Skuas had shot down one bomber and the others had turned away without reaching the convoy. One Skua was lost.

A church service was held on the Sunday we were at sea, the hymn "Eternal Father, Strong to Save" seeming for once appropriate. Afterwards, the Captain addressed the ship's company and told them that *Furious* was going to Belfast for a refit in Harland & Wolff's shipyards. There would be leave in turn for the two watches.

The remainder of the voyage was uneventful and we reached Belfast in the early afternoon. Trucks were waiting for the Army personnel and we were taken to barracks and given ship-and-train passes. We were to take the night boat to Fleetwood, the trucks leaving for the dock at six o'clock.

When we arrived at the boat, I looked out for the Canadian. He was there on the dock and he picked up two large suitcases from a pile of baggage. One he put on his shoulder, hiding his face from the officials checking tickets at the top of the two gangways. I walked up the other one a few yards behind him, had my ticket inspected and turned to see what happened. The two suitcases were taken from him, but he was refused entry and walked back down to the dock.

There were some berths untaken and I was able to book one and went to bed early. Next morning I had breakfast and finished eating just in time to collect my equipment and disembark. Five of us were bound for the Royal Artillery Depot in Woolwich and shared a compartment in the London train. Before it pulled out of the station, the Canadian poked his head in.

"How do I get to Glasgow?"

"Leave this train at Preston and you'll take a Glasgow train there," I was able to tell him. He thanked me and went off. His story did not end there for me, as a month later I saw him asking for help in Charing Cross Station. He was apparently a member in good standing in his unit, for he had a pass and a rail-voucher.

His was as remarkable an escape as that of prisoners of war, though I was surprised to see him free a mere month after reaching England. I would have expected a prison sentence of months rather than weeks for his action.

The journey to Woolwich was expeditious and I was granted a month's leave.

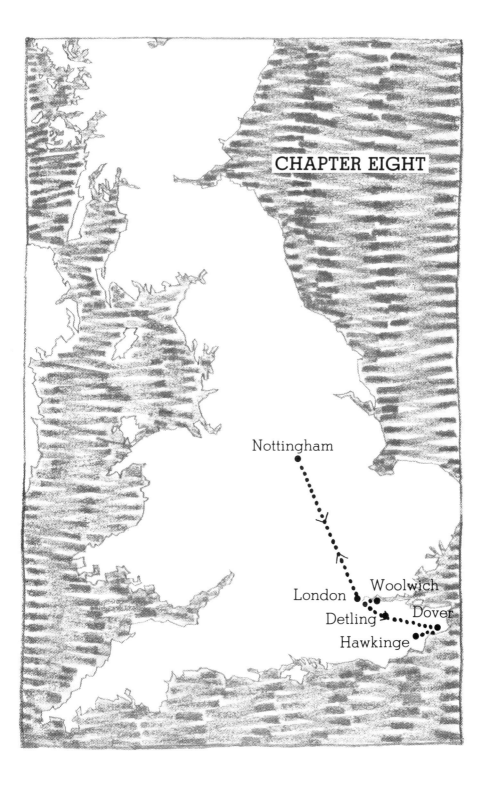

Nottingham

Woolwich

London

Detling

Dover

Hawkinge

CHAPTER 8

ODD JOBS MAN - WITH A NEW GUN

We'll o'er the water, we'll o'er the sea.

James Hogg

Leave over, I reported to the artillery depot at Woolwich. Here, with several hundred others, I waited for a posting to another unit. The recipe for a happy soldier was well understood: on my first day back I was marched with about fifty others to waiting trucks, and in ten minutes I was at a bench in Woolwich Arsenal, the government munitions factory. The work before us was to dismantle the nose-caps of shells which had been damaged by fire when the Arsenal was hit during the "blitz", which still continued. This was a monotonous task, but not dangerous, though it was said the civilians had refused to do it.

The Army tried to give us variety. After a week in the Arsenal, I found myself on a squad armed with picks and shovels. The truck took us to a part of Woolwich where bomb damage had been particularly severe and the remains of houses had to be demolished and removed. We tore down walls still standing and loaded the rubble into trucks. I found I enjoyed standing on a wall and pecking away at the bricks at my feet until they were loosened and fell to the ground. This was succeeded by a less pleasant duty, that of fire-watcher.

Every evening, a bus-load of us, previously warned during morning parade, were detailed to protect Imrie House, a tall white building close to the Tower of London. It was the tallest building in the area, visible for miles on the darkest night and an ideal target for enemy bombers. The buildings on all sides had been razed to the ground. On arrival we were taken up in lifts to the flat roof and the officer in charge gave his speech to the assembled guards:

"You are here to deal with incendiary bombs. They must be attacked as soon as they hit the roof, either covered first with sand or quenched with the stirrup pumps and taken up with the shovels and thrown over the sides. Ten of you will be on duty in two-hour shifts while the others rest in the basement shelter. In the event of an air-raid warning, those below will come up at once to the roof. I will be down below at all times."

This last sentence, meant to be reassuring, indicated to us that nothing could entice him on the roof, certainly not a shower of incendiaries. There were several air-raid warnings on nights when I was on duty but no bombs of any sort were dropped near.

Training as firemen went on at a factory on Woolwich Common, very near the barracks. Here we practised with hoses, rolling them out and using them as quickly as we could on hearing an alarm. We were not required to take shifts during the night, but slept dressed to waste no time if there were an air-raid.

All this training was eventually put to good use. On Saturday, May 11th 1941, I went to London in the evening to see a film. After the show, I was enjoying a drink in a pub when an air-raid began. A man with whom I had been talking invited some of us to go to his flat; we could use the shelter in the basement if the bombing became severe. While we were there the air-raid became very violent and the whole building shook. I thought I'd try to find a way back to Woolwich by train, tram or bus. Outside, the noise of bombs, planes and anti-aircraft batteries firing from Hyde Park made the night nerve-racking and the fire and smoke leaping up above the buildings on all sides were hideous. The air was pungent with the smell of burning wood, rubber and paint. I decided that it was most unlikely I could find public transport going to Woolwich, and fell in with a small crew of firemen trundling a small pumper. Undermanned, they welcomed me. Their job was to go into houses where incendiary bombs had fallen through the roof and had set fire to the attic. To effect this, the hose was taken up to the top of the house after the pumper had been coupled to a hydrant. If the fire was brought under control, the bomb could be brought out of the house. The danger in this procedure occurred when the fire had burnt through the attic floor - the water tank would crash through and land on the top flight of stairs - just where the man with the hose would be standing. By morning, the fires in the pumper's area of operation were out and I left with a note from the fireman in charge, saying that I had been working all night with his unit.

On my way to the Embankment, I passed the Queen's Hall, where I had often been to concerts, most recently during my leave. It was a shell and still smouldering. I walked in to view the damage. The lower part of the building was dripping with water but the fire had destroyed it beyond repair. The damage was great throughout the West End, and, when I caught a bus, I saw the House of Commons, badly damaged in the raid. In terms of human injuries and deaths, this was the worst of all raids on London.

The depot at Woolwich had been hit by several bombs. I reported in and was noted as having survived. It had been decided to move the depot to Nottingham because of the damage, caused by this most recent raid as well as earlier attacks. Before the move, however, we took part in a huge parade to aid a War Savings drive which the town of Woolwich had organized. We marched past the Mayor and on through the town. On the way back I was in the last row and, as we rounded a very sharp curve, dropped out to tie my bootlace. By the time I had untied it in order to tie it up again, the parade was out of sight. By an amazing coincidence I happened to be by a bus stop, just as the bus, which would take me to my mother's house, arrived. I was soon home.

The move to Nottingham was quick and easy. Houses very near the Gooses Fair grounds were our billet, and the city became very popular with the troops. Girls from the tobacco and bicycle factories thronged the pubs, played darts expertly, and "Pushed out the boat" in their turn. It was here that I broke the Army's unwritten rule which said, positively and coarsely, "Never volunteer for anything." It happened one Friday night that a party of us were late returning after evening leave. As we turned the corner to our billets, there the Orderly Bombardier and two "Red-caps" waited. They took our names and warned us that we would be on charge next day. On the following morning's parade a volunteer was called for, and, on impulse, I stepped forward.

"Report to the Orderly Room," said the sergeant. I walked across and entered the office. Nobody was in so I shuffled my feet noisily to gain attention. Still nobody came, and to while

52

away the time I looked over the large pile of "fizzers", Army slang for Form 252, the Charge Sheet. I quickly leafed through until I came to my own, "6792294, Gunner Waters, S." I put it in my pocket and coughed loudly. Eventually somebody came and showed me the piles of documents I was to carry to another room.

After a few weeks in Nottingham, I was sent to nearby Bestwood Lodge, popularly supposed to have been a hunting lodge in Sherwood Forest. Here the Army kept a permanent guard over the house, which was empty, and the grounds, which were neglected and overgrown. Nobody knew why it was guarded. The building was old and rat-infested. One of the guards had a set of scissors, clippers and combs for haircutting but was afraid to use them. He lent them to me and I had a good business for the rest of my stay.

From here I was posted to a light anti-aircraft battery stationed in Kent, not far from a fighter aerodrome near the village of Detling. The Battery was not operational but its purpose was to train gunners for the Bofors gun. This gun, a Swedish invention, was being produced in great numbers in England to counter the German dive-bomber Junkers 87, known as the "Stuka." These bombers had proved a devastating weapon in the defeat of Poland and France. The Bofors gun had a calibre - that is, barrel diameter - of 40 mm., about one and three-quarter inches. The shells, which weighed about two pounds each, came in clips of five, and the gun fired either at single shot or automatic with a rate of 120 rounds a minute. It was aimed by two layers with large ring sights, one layer controlling the elevation, raising or lowering the barrel, while the other controlled the bearing, moving the gun left or right. Working together the two layers could follow the target, leading it to compensate for speed, much as a shotgun is used to shoot birds or clay pigeons. Two or three gunners handed up the clips of shells to the loader, who placed them in a slide. After the gun was cocked by the loading handle, the loader could set the gun to fire single shots with each depression of the firing pedal, or to fire at automatic by keeping his foot down. A good team of ammunition handlers and loader could maintain the gun at 120 rounds per minute. The Bofors had a spring-loaded carriage which, when opened, raised the front and rear wheels and lowered the gun to the ground, where it rested on four pads. Large picket pins secured the carriage to the ground to give it a firm position.

Our mentor was a young man, Sergeant Pike, who worked us very hard in the necessary drills at which we were all beginners. The camp-site was remote and there was nowhere to go, even for an evening leave. For a diversion the sergeant had erected some straw-filled sacks, on which we practised bayonet drill till our bared-teeth hatred of the dummies satisfied him. An inspecting officer came to see us at drill and promised us leave when we were proficient.

From Detling, we went to a gun-site near Dover where we continued our training, but were also operational and saw something of the cross-Channel shelling. The German shells landed on Dover while our reply was made by guns concealed in a railway tunnel. The guns came out of the tunnel on railway lines, fired, and were hauled back. I was given a week's leave which I spent with my wife in a quiet part of north Wales, near Denbigh.

Another move, just after my return from leave, took us to Hawkinge to help defend the fighter base from which Spitfires and Hurricanes were making sweeps into northern France. There were occasional retaliatory raids by the Luftwaffe and we had many "Stand-to's" but no planes came within range. Our training now was concentrated on the mobile use of the Bofors gun.

To this end, we went to Acrise Manor, a house of considerable age, situated in a wall-enclosed area, pierced by a roofed archway. The enclosure also contained a small farmhouse and stables. The exercises in mobility were planned as map reading tests for the troop commanders and, sometimes, for the sergeants in charge of the detachments. During the day we would have to find the chosen gun position and bring the gun into action as quickly as possible. After an officer had checked that we were effectively in action and had hidden or camouflaged our gun tower, an order to move to another location would reach us, whereupon we had to pack and race to the new spot, where we went through the same routines. I learned on a very wet day that the tow-er - a Morris vehicle with a six-wheel chassis, two back wheels in line at the rear on each side - had a great propensity to become bogged down in the mud. The rearmost wheel only on either side was driven; if it couldn't move the tractor forward, it merely dug ever deeper into the mud. We often returned to the old manor wet, muddy and tired.

One night I had a very frightening experience which, at the time, I thought was a bad nightmare. I felt an overpowering evil presence which hung over me, much as a dark cloud might. Three years later, in Cairo, I read an account of the manor in a Forces paper in which the writer had had a similar experience. He had made inquiries locally and was told that the manor was haunted. Again, many years later in conversation with a friend, a distinguished flyer in World War One, I learned that he had stayed at Acrise Manor, and had experienced the same strong fear of evil. I should have known that Army food rarely causes nightmares.

PART FOUR

LIVERPOOL - DURBAN - BENGHAZI, 1941

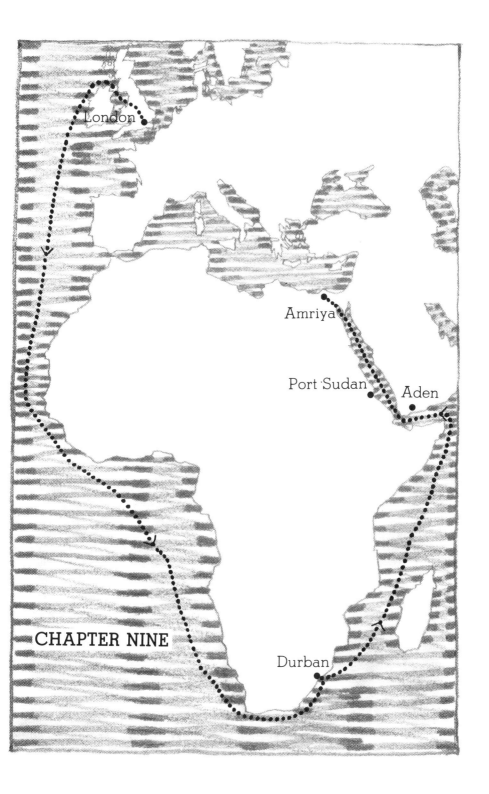

CHAPTER NINE

CHAPTER 9

THE WAR AGAIN - THIRD TIME LUCKY?

Sad to say I'm on my way, Shan't be back for many a day.

trad. Jamaican song

Our training now complete, we left Acrise Manor and returned to Hawkinge.

Three of us were awakened at 4:00 a.m. one morning early in September. A truck waited while we packed up our entire kit. We were taken to Battery Headquarters where a sleepy clerk handed us our travel warrants and orders which told us to report to a light anti-aircraft battery with the First Armoured Division. The truck deposited us at the railway station and a train took us to London. Here I telephoned my wife and she came to Paddington Station where we were to board the train for Swindon. I concluded there would be no more leave for a long while, as the most likely destination for an armoured division at that time - September 1941 - was the Middle East. We said goodbye. I would not see my wife again until March 1945.

The draft consisted of Gunners Black, Brown and Waters. Walter Brown, often called "Topper" or "WTW" (his initials), became a great friend, even an invaluable one. Black was a dour Scot, a very self-contained one; although we were usually in different gun detachments, because of our being sent together to a new unit on this particular day, he was always more than a mere acquaintance. Later I learned that Brown's home was in Malvern, where my wife was living, and she was able to meet his family and exchange news from our letters home.

Transport was waiting for us at Swindon and took us to the battery's camp in the Marlborough Downs. We were given our tent space, and instantly I was offered a drink by a tall, dark young man with slanted, impish eyes. His name was Alan Bellamy. The battery we were joining had fought in France with the 51st Highland Division, and many of the men - including Bellamy - had been captured at St. Valery-en-Caux, near Dieppe. He had escaped on the line of march, cycled through France on his own, and crossed the Pyrenees into Spain. Here he had been interned in horrible conditions in a prison, where he had languished for several months before the British Consul had secured his release. He was taken to Gibraltar (at the time I was there), and returned to the United Kingdom. He could have remained in England for the rest of the war, but had signed a disclaimer of this privilege extended to escaped prisoners, in order to go overseas again with his regiment. His service in France and mine in Norway and Gibraltar forged an instant bond between us.

The final preparations being made for departure, I requested embarkation leave. This was refused; there was no time. Although I did not know it, this turned out to be a great advantage later, as it left my foreign service record unbroken from the date of my departure for Norway, which resulted in leave and pay benefits at the end of the War. It was less than six months since I had returned from Gibraltar when we left Liverpool docks on September 21st 1941, bound for Egypt.

The S.S. *Samaria* was the first converted troop ship I had sailed on. There were about three thousand men on board, sleeping in hammocks slung above the mess tables where we ate our meals. Even with the huge canvas ventilators, long funnels rigged to allow fresh air from above deck to improve the atmosphere below, the conditions were most unpleasant - stuffy and malodorous. Many of us, fortunately, were able to sling our hammocks in the open but covered deck below the boat deck. I did this after just one night down below. It was chilly in the North Atlantic but I slept warm and soundly. Thus the congestion was relieved below and the atmosphere greatly improved for meals. As usual I was seasick for a few hours on the first day only; thereafter even the stormy weather rounding the Cape of Good Hope did not upset me.

Courses in semaphore and map reading, lectures on all aspects of desert living, and bouts of physical training helped while away the days.

There was time for recreation and Bellamy and I indulged a common liking for chess. More vigorous activity occurred in a boxing ring, erected on the boat deck. A competition was organized for all units, and our battery was well represented. Several of our better fighters were brought up from the ship's cells where, for various offences aboard, they had been confined. The fly-weight final was fought between two of our gunners, a Jock from Glasgow who had been boxing professionally for years, with the flattened nose and cauliflower ears to prove it, and Benjy. Benjy, a battery clerk, was a Jew. He was a slight, unassuming little man who wore glasses. It came as a surprise that he had even entered the competition, yet here he was in the final of his class! He did not look the part, but for the three rounds he calmly held off the Scot - who never stopped punching - without once retreating. It was a triumph of mind over muscle.

The blackout each night made for an early hammock-time, especially after "crossing the line"; the heat of the equator, when experienced on a crowded troop ship, proved only a little less than unbearable!

At Cape Town half the convoy of troop ships and escorts went to dock for a week's furlough while our half continued to Durban where we were to spend our leave. It was a welcome respite in so attractive a city. The service men's clubs were a haven for us poorly-paid combatants; the array of fresh fruits I particularly enjoyed, and the excellent facilities for games. Elsewhere, Durban's zoo was exceptionally interesting, the swimming from the beaches was the finest most of us had ever known, and the best cinema was air-conditioned, with a ceiling like a star-lit sky, across which white clouds seemed to pass! I saw two very good films there, Leslie Howard in *Pimpernel Smith* and Spencer Tracy in *Dr. Jekyll and Mr. Hyde*.

Several of us were shopping for gifts to send home one morning. As we walked along, occupying most of the pavement, some natives came towards us. I was by the curb and naturally thought nothing of stepping into the road. A moment later a white South African rushed up to me, his face red with rage.

"How are we going to live here if you do that?"

"What did I do?" I asked, not understanding.

"You stepped off the pavement for those niggers," he shouted. "It's for them to step off for you!"

I could think of nothing to say. On another occasion, while on the way to the zoo, we caught a bus and, ignorant of the rules, sat down in the section reserved for natives. The conductor was angry and told us to move to the white part of the bus or get off. We wondered what would happen to a native who made such a mistake.

Most of us could no longer afford the fleshpots by the end of our week's stay, and - fortunately perhaps - the voyage resumed. One entertainment, by no means official, and which had happened before our stop at Durban and continued after it, remained a mystery. Somebody, obviously a fan of Leslie Charteris's books about "The Saint", habitually defecated in the baths in the officers' quarters in the cabins on the top decks. Each offering was accompanied by a card, bearing a stick-man figure and neatly labelled "The Shitter strikes again." The news circulated swiftly each time it happened, and everyone - with the exception of the officers - enjoyed the success of the perpetrator and his ability to avoid capture. He never was caught.

A vastly different diversion was provided by the offer of prizes for the best essays about our recent leave. This interested me, especially when I recalled that my father had enjoyed a similar stay in 1901 while serving in the Boer War. I wrote about a typical leave that I might have had, but concluded, "thus it was that my father in 1901 enjoyed leave in Durban." I won a prize, a very large bucket of beer, around which eight of us sat with mugs and drank.

Shortly after leaving Durban part of the convoy headed for Singapore, including the battleship *Repulse*. The other ships, bound for Port Suez, lined up in two columns and cheered as they passed between. Two months later Singapore was in Japanese hands, and the *Repulse* had been sunk.

At Aden our anchors were dropped, but there was no shore leave, to our disappointment, because Aden was under quarantine for an epidemic. We were allowed to visit Port Sudan for three hours in the afternoon. It was very hot and smelly. Most interesting to me were the huge heads of hair on the dock workers, reminiscent of the battles in the Sudan with the Mahdi and his "Fuzzie-wuzzies." Port Suez was reached in two days and we went into camp not far from town. This was the staging point for disembarking troops and the length of stay was usually not more than two days. We were there for one night and it gave us an opportunity to sample the open-air cinemas. High bamboo-like walls enclosed a sandy patch with backless wooden benches facing the screen. The films were old, but added interest was inadvertently given the three-reelers by showing the final reel in place of the second, which tended to steer a film to an inconclusive end.

The next morning a troop train awaited us. It wandered all day through the length and breadth of Egypt. We saw many thousands of Italian prisoners of war in their compounds; they had been rounded up during the first desert campaign in 1940. Surprising was the belligerent attitude of many of them. Even more surprising was the first visit to the train's sanitary facilities; at first sight an empty room, a second look revealed an empty room with a rectangular hole in the floor! This was the complete facility. The wooden benches were hard, and by evening we were tired. The train skirted Alexandria, reached the coast and finally stopped at Amriya, our destination.

CHAPTER 10

DESERT TENDERFOOTS

The sea-like, pathless, limitless waste of sand.
Henry Wadsworth Longfellow

The Army wasted no time once we arrived in Amriya. On the first morning I was marched into the battery commander's office and promoted to bombardier...two stripes at once! Alan Bellamy became sergeant, and I was put in his detachment. The drivers went off to Alexandria and came back with guns and trucks. Next day they returned to Alexandria to have the trucks painted the colour of the desert. All was done with great dispatch.

We were instructed about the four German aircraft we were likely to see. Two were fighters, the Messerschmidt F109, a single-engine plane comparable to the Spitfire, and the Messerschmidt 110, a two-engine machine also used as a light bomber. The two bombers were the Junkers 87, a single-engine dive-bomber which had caused havoc in Poland and France, and the Junkers 88, a two-engine medium bomber which carried four 250-pound bombs. Both bombers had lattice diving-brakes which screamed loudly, scare tactics which had added to their effectiveness in the campaigns in Europe. The Junkers 88s in the desert were normally used in compact formations of twenty-four and dropped their bombs simultaneously. This "pattern-bombing" was frightening, but caused surprisingly little damage if the vehicles being attacked were properly dispersed. The Junkers 87s bombed by diving very steeply, brakes screaming, and releasing their bombs as they pulled out of their dives. They were susceptible to determined Bofors' fire, the tracer shells being visible to the pilots who would often pull out without bombing, or turn aside in evasion.

While the equipment was being readied, we learned the ways of life in Egypt. The speed of the *dhobi*, for example, the laundryman who collected your clothes at breakfast and delivered them by lunch, dry, starched and pressed. Experience taught us not to stray away on dark nights. Many on guard were lost a few yards from their tents or trucks and lay down to sleep on the ground until first light. We learned to drink the local beer, said to be made from onion skins. A few words of Arabic were picked up and it seemed the less literate gunners were more adept than the better educated.

By Christmas Day 1941 all was in order for the battle. We were going to relieve the famous Seventh Armoured Division, the Desert Rats, who were still harrying the retreating Germans and Italians.

Turkey was on the menu for dinner, but it was not a festive occasion. Rain poured all day. Our possessions, including bedding, were packed and stowed in the vehicles. I had a three-ton truck with half the detachment, while Alan Bellamy was with the gun, gun tow-er and the rest of the gunners. I dozed in front of the truck till we set out, at 4 a.m. on December 26th.

The first leg of our march was along the coast road. We travelled in a single column with one hundred yards between vehicles. The surface was good and we made excellent progress. There was little of interest and Driver Lomax was glad to doze for a while, and I content to drive.

Before our first day's march was over we had left the road and were fairly into the desert. It was a surprise to most of us that it was not sandy. There was some sand where it had blown around the small scrub bushes or gathered in shallow patches in depressions. Mostly the desert is stony and rocky, often hard on the vehicles' springs.

The orders for a large formation, when travelling in the desert, call for the guns, gun tow-ers and trucks to be formed up in a convenient number of columns, spaced about one hundred yards apart, with the same distance between the columns. At the front of the middle column is the leader of the formation, who provides signals for starting and stopping. A blue flag is held up from the leader's vehicle indicating that engines should be started, all equipment loaded and guns taken out of action and

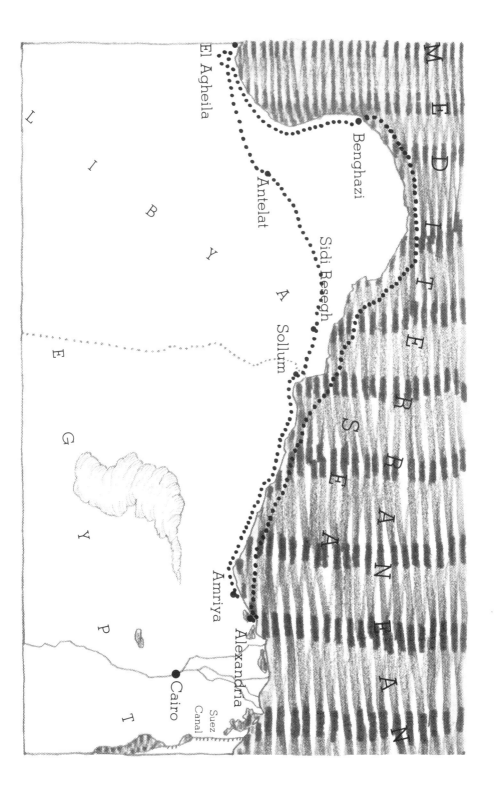

attached to their tow-ers. When the flag is lowered, the formation moves forward. Officers of the units which make up the formation are expected to see that all vehicles maintain the correct distances. This is the best protection against bombers.

At the end of a day's march, the evening meal is cooked and eaten while the vehicles are stopped in the wide-spread formation. Then, just after sunset, the whole formation moves off again slowly, the columns closing in towards the centre until they are about five yards apart. At the same time, each column closes until the vehicles are nose to tail. This is the close "laager" used during hours of darkness. Each morning the process is reversed. The vehicles move out to the one hundred yard spacing before dawn. Then breakfast is taken. No set stop takes place for a noon meal.

We had much to learn, not only about movement on the march, but regarding the mechanism of feeding the unit. A troop consists of about forty-five men, made up of four gun detachments of ten men, and five or six in Troop Headquarters. The whole troop is fed together during training. On active service this is not possible. The rations must be divided to feed separately each of the gun detachments and the headquarters. Food is almost all tinned goods: butter, cheese, jam, milk, bacon, bully beef, vegetables and stew. How to divide three tins of jam five ways, without containers and kitchen utensils? Our troop sergeant, Harry Nayland, was incorruptible and absolutely fair.

I was always hungry, though I was probably better fed than most, for Lomax did not like Army biscuits. He gave them to me, and I munched slowly as we bumped over the desert. With drink we did better. Our water ration gave us a large mug of tea morning and evening, and an occasional "buckshee" brew-up during the day. To make the tea or cook the food, the bottom six inches of a four-gallon petrol can was filled with sand, soaked with petrol and lit. A dixie would boil in about four minutes.

The desert was clean and, unless we stayed more than three days in one place, we never saw a fly. A few inches of water sufficed for shaving; some even sacrificed two inches of tea for that. As we were moving every day, there was no time to build latrines. In turn we would take the detachment spade and find a sandy spot well away from the truck. While squatting on one such expedition, I saw a piece of green blotting paper clinging to a scrubby bush. I retrieved it and, seeing that it had been used to blot

66

something written in German, I decided not to put it to the use I had proposed for it, but to give it to my troop officer. I was commended for my action!

We settled down and learned quickly the ways of desert living. Soon we reached the battlefield of the fierce fighting of the autumn of 1941. We climbed the pass at Halfaya and crossed the wide belt of wire which the Italians had erected at the frontier between Egypt and Libya. We passed through the wreckage of the fighting at Sidi Omar, Sidi Resegh and Gambut, hard-fought battles as the burnt out trucks, tanks and airplanes testified. In some cases the dead had been buried where they fell.

Some of our vehicles needed maintenance and we stopped near Bir Gobi, roughly south of Tobruk. To me fell the task of taking a gun tow-er to the workshops to have a broken leaf-spring repaired. This involved navigation in the featureless desert, comparable to a sea voyage. Our destination was eight miles away on a magnetic bearing of seventy-five degrees. The bearing had to be taken on the compass some twenty yards from the vehicle since it would be influenced by the metal. At the end of eight miles we found from a nearby unit that the workshops had moved and were seven miles away, the bearing now one hundred and five degrees. We navigated this and found our objective. While we waited we were fed generously on a porridge of biscuit, bully beef and cheese, a desert staple diet. It was getting near dusk when the work was finished and I asked for a direct bearing back to our laager. This proved to be two hundred and sixty degrees at twelve miles. We hurried to race the darkness and drove straight to the place in the laager that we had left that morning, just as the blue flag was raised to call us in for the night.

From Bir Gobi we moved somewhat south of west and no longer stayed roughly parallel to the coast, but cut inland across the bulge of Libya. Usually we were on the stony Sahara, but occasionally we descended a steep wadi and raced across a flat, cracked mud-pan which may have been dry for many years. Once we saw the classic sight in a desert, the wind and sand-scoured bones of the skeleton of a camel.

Our march was quiet and continued until we were again near the coast. We stopped at Antelat where we took water from the "well-with-the-wind-pump", a famous landmark known to all who ever passed that way. Our division had by now completely relieved the Seventh, and only an expanse of desert separated us from the enemy. At this time the fashion in desert fighting was "Jock Columns", named after Brigadier Jock Campbell, V.C., a legendary hero of the 1941 campaigns. The columns comprised the anti-tank and anti-aircraft Bofors, 25-pounder field guns and a hit-and-run tactic to surprise the enemy and escape before retaliation.

We left Antelat and its famous well and held our westerly course. That evening, after we had eaten and gone into laager for the night, I walked to Battery Headquarters to visit Walter Brown. We sat in his truck and chatted over a tin of pineapple from a Church Army canteen, always the foremost Christian outpost. It was an intensely dark moonless night and my friend was worried. How can you find your way back, half a mile or more? Easily, I just follow a star, the Pole Star. He was ashamed that he could not recognize it in the starlit sky. I showed him and found my way back.

Next morning Lt. Mackie took me aside and told me he was very worried about Sgt. Halton. I was to join the sergeant's gun-team in case he should break down. I gathered up my possessions and walked across to join my new crew while Lance-Bombardier Holland, the troop clerk, took charge of my truck. Holland was a pleasant, quiet man, liked by all.

A few minutes after this exchange the flag went up in the lead vehicle to warn us of an imminent move. The gun was taken out of action, the gun tow-er backed on to it, the trail eye hooked up and we moved off.

The going was difficult. We were in the Wadi Faragh area, a wide river which, on rare occasions, became a raging torrent, but was now a sea of sand. Towing a gun in such conditions needed the sand-channels, two six-foot lengths of steel about a foot wide punched with small holes to grip the surface. These were placed in front of the drive wheels of the tow-er after the gun had been detached. The vehicle then drove over the channels as quickly as possible to gain momentum. The channels were then rushed forward and replaced as soon as the tow-er stopped. When this had taken it about the length of the tow-rope away from the gun, the tow was run out to the gun and the winch pulled it up to the tow-er. This was slow, exhausting work.

Sgt. Halton thought he was best occupied driving the gun tow-er, which left me in charge of the sand-channel operation. We slogged away for an hour. It had been a cold January morning, but it grew hotter and I threw my coat and cap into the vehicle. Our last winching brought the gun up a steep slope where Halton, already stuck in the sand, was trying to blast out by racing the engine until it screamed and then letting the clutch in with a bang.

Now on top of the slope, for the first time I became aware of machine-gun and shell fire. About twenty yards away I saw an officer, field glasses raised to his eyes, standing on the roof of a shooting-brake command car. I looked in the same direction as he and saw with the naked eye German tanks, seven or eight hundred yards away, moving straight towards us, firing as they came. A shell burst alongside the command car without doing any apparent damage to it, or to us. In the next moment I realized that not only German tanks, but also our own bren-carriers were hurrying towards us, the latter in retreat.

Unfortunately, Field Marshal Rommel had chosen this day to launch a major offensive and we were caught, a bit of meat on the end of a spear!

Meanwhile Sgt. Halton was still racing the engine, though no drive was being transmitted to the wheels. The clutch, transmission, or both were wrecked. This the sergeant was reluctant to believe. Without our tow-er we were helpless except to wait for death or capture. The sergeant, preoccupied with the vehicle, seemed unaware of the precarious situation. I could not see any of our troop's guns, nor the troop commander, but before making a decision which now appeared to devolve on me, I found help at hand. At that moment a Rifle Brigade bren-carrier stopped and the driver asked if we needed help. I explained our predicament and he said the carrier could tow the gun. With some help I manhandled the gun into position and the rest of the detachment scrambled on the carrier. Sgt. Halton abandoned the truck and joined the others, while a gunner and I rode on the gun.

We moved off in full retreat. It was at once plain that, in my haste, I had used an unnecessarily long tow. The gun-trail kept digging in the sand or catching up and hitting the carrier. A young, dark Welshman, Gunner Pugh, and I had a rough ride and I was terrified the gun would roll over. The carrier stopped eventually. We shortened the tow and Pugh and I joined the others. I had to cling on by my eyebrows. Every time I tried to improve my position, I burnt a buttock on the engine cover.

By now we had outstripped the tanks, but the Stukas were adding to the dangers of our headlong retreat. The going was firmer but bumpy and the gun finally rolled over. It could no longer be towed so Sgt. Halton "spiked" it, to deny its use to the enemy, while I undid the tow. We went on and again the Stukas came, their lattice air-brakes screaming as they released bombs while diving steeply at us, looking like demented hawks.

What Lt. Mackie had foreseen now happened. Sgt. Halton began to shout incoherently. He managed to rise momentarily on the swaying carrier screaming that he couldn't stand it. He jumped from the back of the vehicle and rolled over and over. I shouted to the driver but could not make him hear, nor could I move nearer. I doubt if any of the carrier crew knew what had happened and we continued our flight.

We met a three-ton truck of the Rifle Brigade and stopped to talk things over. It was then I learned that the sergeant in command of the bren-carrier had seen his friend in another carrier killed and the shock had caused him to lose his power of speech. I asked him to write down his name and number so I could report his crew's rescue of us. His name was Vann. Much later I learned that he had been captured when a field dressing station was overrun by the Germans. All wounded who could walk were taken prisoner, while the medical personnel, their ambulances and the stretcher-cases were allowed to try to regain the British lines.

It was agreed that we should travel with the truck. Halton had left his coat, belt, pistol and prismatic compass on the carrier, so I took possession of them, sergeant's stripes included, before it drove off. That night we slept under a tarpaulin, but it was bitterly cold without blankets.

We reached the coast road to Benghazi early next morning and were stopped by the Military Police. We were told to report to the transit camp in Benghazi. There we were fed and provided with the bare necessities - blankets, tooth brush - to replace what we had left on the tow-er. An intelligence officer asked me for an account of the previous day's happenings. He told me that as soon as the dust and confusion settled down we would be sent to our unit. In the meantime, I was given a labour force of two huge guardsmen and instructed to tidy up the grounds.

We were sent on our way next morning, once more with the riflemen in their truck, only to be ordered back again to Benghazi; the German advance had already reached the destination given in our orders.

On the evening of the second day of our stay we were paraded and marched down to the docks. There we boarded a small merchant ship already packed with civilian refugees, mostly Jewish families. Two other vessels made up the convoy - an oil tanker and a Royal Navy escort ship, somewhat smaller and more lightly armed than a destroyer.

Darkness had fallen as we cleared the harbour and the ships wallowed in a very rough sea. The Army personnel taking passage were given an empty part of the hold. We reached it by a twenty foot descent down a set of rungs screwed to the wall. By the time I had taken my turn and reached the bottom, I was feeling very sick and became oblivious to the danger of falling over the unprotected edge of the hold into the depths below. I vomited until I fell asleep.

The high seas had not abated when I emerged from the hold next morning. The deck space and hatch covers were crowded with refugees. Overnight a woman had given birth. The food supplies we had brought had almost all been stolen. Seconds after my reaching the deck, a sergeant of the Royal Engineers told me to report to the officer-in-charge of troops, who was on the boat deck. The officer ordered me to man the two Marlin machine-guns there with my detachment and to keep two look-outs posted. I was still very seasick as I pushed my way through the refugees to round up my men.

It was pleasant on the boat deck, servicing the guns for action. I even managed to eat some Army biscuit, nutritious though no gourmet's choice.

We had been working for some time before I noticed that one ship was no longer with our convoy.

"What happened to the tanker?" I asked a ship's officer.

"Torpedoed last night," was the laconic reply.

After a fleeting vision of the packed hold, the single ladder and the lack of any lifebelts, I decided to sleep on deck in future.

The alarm sounded while we were still struggling with the machine-guns. From the boat deck we had a grandstand view of an Italian bomber trying to sink the escort vessel with its torpedoes. The ship heeled wildly as it made violent turns to dodge the attacks. Twice the bomber missed and then flew close alongside us, machine-gunning. So near was the plane that we could plainly see the crew. All the soldiers with rifles lined the deck and fired at the enemy. I shot at the bomber with the sergeant's revolver and the bullets from the plane twanged in the rigging above and punctured the funnel.

There were no more attacks and we reached Tobruk. We had expected to put in there, but were ordered to continue eastwards and in the afternoon of the next day we entered the harbour of Alexandria. Trucks took us to a pleasant camp on the east side towards Aboukir. We were in sight and sound of the sea a few yards away across the Corniche, the coast road.

CHAPTER 11

BACK TO THE DRAWING-BOARD...
IN A HURRY

War is little more than a catalogue of mistakes and misfortunes.
Winston Churchill

The camp was called Mustapha Barracks. It had a core of permanent buildings and a tent area, a necessary addition since Alexandria had become the main supply base for the desert war. There was also a railway line to Mersa Matruh which was now being rapidly extended towards Tobruk.

Our great concern was to rejoin our battery, but the orderly room staff told us that until our unit's position was known and there was a large enough draft of reinforcements to justify a troop train, we would have to possess our souls in patience. However a pay parade helped to make the delay more bearable, and we were given a few duties - "fatigues" the Army aptly calls them - which passed the time.

When we finally entrained, we were dismayed to learn that our destination was a transit camp at Mersa Matruh. Our movement orders did not spell out a return to our unit. On arrival, the officer-in-charge reported us into the camp, which consisted of row upon row of tents in the open desert. An Army bathhouse mobile unit was set up nearby, a contraption of racks of shower heads and canvas screens, with duck boards for a floor, a fruitful source of splinters. To our surprise, one of our battery trucks was parked nearby. I called out to the driver.

"Where's the Battery?"

He looked up, recognized me and spoke.

"Thought you were dead."

As an afterthought he continued, "The mob's just down there" - and pointed - "about three hundred yards."

I rushed off and explained to the camp commander that I wanted to return to my unit and take the rest of the detachment with me. No objection was made so we shouldered our belongings and set off.

Our reception was enthusiastic and "Smudger" Smith, the battery clerk, complained that he had reported me "Missing, believed captured" and now he would have to alter everything. Happily, the list had not gone forward. Walter Brown came running and shook my hand. I'd saved his life, he said. He had remembered all about the Pole Star and had driven his truck to safety, packed with strays from our own and other units who had lost their transport.

Lt. Mackie, who always worried greatly about his men's safety and well-being, was very pleased to see us back. He told me I was promoted to lance-sergeant, and to full sergeant unless Sgt. Halton turned up. In any case, I was to command the gun detachment.

Not all the news was good. Two hours after taking over my truck, Lance-Bombarbier Holland had been shot by heavy machine-gun fire from a tank. The driver had lifted him from the truck and Holland had died urging the driver to leave him. Lomax had stayed for the few remaining moments and had reached safety.

Alan Bellamy took me into the "Sergeants' Mess" - a large hole, with a roof, dug into a sand dune. I luckily had enough money to "push out the boat" in order to "wet my stripes." By the end of the evening they had been baptised by total immersion!

Before going into the Mess, I had been issued with and had erected a small bivouac tent which the Battery now possessed. The tents held two, and usually a hole was dug so they were a foot or so below ground level to protect against draughts. As a sergeant I did not have to share, and mine held all my kit. When I returned from the Mess, it had been knocked down. I was re-erecting it when Gunner Cobbett came past.

"You, a sergeant!" he jeered. "If you were on fire I wouldn't piss on you to put you out."

Cobbett was a good gunner. His own sergeant had been wounded, and disappointment at not being promoted - and beer - had no doubt caused his expression of resentment at my promotion.

74

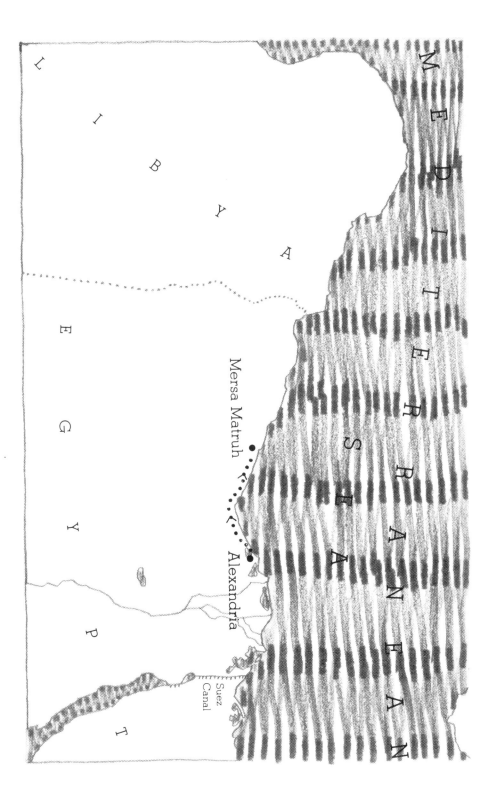

Next morning Lt. Mackie told me that the Battery was changing its organization from three troops of four guns each to four troops of three guns. This made it easier to give anti-aircraft protection to four units without causing administrative problems. He was to be commander of the new "D" Troop.

My gun detachment was then chosen. My Number Two was Bombardier Cooper, a Regular Army soldier who would be a great help maintaining the gun and its equipment. I was to have my friend Walter Brown. This delighted me. Gunners Stacey and Venables - who, because of poor eyesight, had first been drafted to the Pioneer Corps, but had managed to transfer to the Artillery - were next added to my team. They were inseparable friends, never complained, shirked nothing and showed no fear in action. Both were physically large and strong. To complete the detachment were Gunners Whalley, Walker, Mason (the driver), and Howson (the cook). Later Lance-Bombarbier Fletcher, from Wigan, was added. I had hoped to have a gunner named Vesey, a friend of Stacey and Venables and of the same type. Unfortunately, he had spoken with one of Sgt. Halton's detachment, who had bluntly informed him, "Don't go with him; that bastard will have you all killed!"

Vesey, unfortunately, took this to mean that when action was imminent, instead of firing, the detachment would dive for cover till the planes had passed. As a result, he joined another detachment.

New gun tow-ers arrived for "D". These were Bedfords with four-wheel drive, a welcome improvement after our exertions with the sand-channels in our last adventures. The Bedfords were taller than our previous tow-ers and therefore more visible to the enemy, but their ability to move through sand more than made up for this. At first we had trouble with their penchant for boiling up very quickly. We eventually solved this problem by taking off the doors of the driver's cab, the engine cover and the windshield. This so improved the air cooling that we no longer had to use our precious water supply for the radiator.

Our first trial with the new tow-er nearly ended in total disaster. We tried it on the silver sands of Matruh and were pleased with its ability to move easily in the deepest sand. As we decided to return, the driver turned towards the sea and ran into a patch of water-soaked sand... Quicksand! The tow-er sank on the seaward side until it rested on its chassis and body. We drove in the pickets which held the ground anchor and tried to winch the tow-er out, but in vain. Finally it was extricated by two other tow-ers, coming free with a tremendous squelch.

There was no doubt that our knowledge of the desert had greatly increased as a result of our first experience. We were much more confident now, which was fortunate, because clearly we would soon be going back. All equipment was in order, the Battery was up to strength, and, in all ways, ready.

PART FIVE
TOBRUK, 1942

CHAPTER 12

INTO BATTLE...

Then never let me crouch against the wall,
But meet my fears and fight them till I fall.

Sidney Keyes

Our march to the concentration areas used the coast road. Instead of bumping up the Halfaya Pass, we travelled the very steep ascent at Sollum, on a good paved road. The railway had now been laid within twenty miles of Tobruk and was put to great use, as goods trains were bringing up supplies in huge quantities from Alexandria, a saving in time and in petrol over the usual convoy of trucks.

It was here at railhead that my gun and its men were adopted by the South African railway engineers, who looked after the rolling stock. Each night all of us, except one gunner on guard, were invited to their mess tent to hear the B.B.C. news and have a cup of coffee. We were interested to hear from these experts that steam engines need good water and that this commodity, brought up from Alexandria, was always available at railhead for the return journey of the engines. The kind South Africans kept us well supplied, and we were able to wash ourselves and our clothes without sacrificing our own skimpy supply.

To anyone who knows the mysterious ways of the Army it was obvious that these idyllic conditions would not long continue. One day Lt. Mackie came to us in a great hurry. We were to take our gun out of action and follow him. Our course went alongside the railway, some ten miles from railhead, where a Messerschmidt 109 was attacking an engine hauling a train. Before we could bring the gun into action, the plane had gone. Unfortunately, it was decided to leave us there in case the same place was used for further sorties against the trains.

We had put the gun in a patch of scrub, rather taller than usual, inadvertently camouflaging it from ground observation. Frequently, after nearly colliding with it, officers congratulated us on the effectiveness of the concealment.

We had acquired a seat from an Army latrine, to which we hinged a cover. Since we might have a lengthy stay, we dug a hole, sandbagged above it to a convenient height, and installed the seat. It so happened that the place where we had been able to dig was very much in the open, with a good view of the railway track. An opinion often advanced was that the gun and the seat might, to save embarrassment, usefully change places.

There had been no opportunity during our first trip to fire our guns. Of all the guns in the Battery, it fell to mine to engage the enemy for the first time. One particularly dark night, after all the men except the guard were in bed, a German intruder - probably a Junkers 88 - was heard quite low and very close. It went away, but Walter Brown, who was on guard, thought it might return. He called me, Stacey and Venables, and we manned the gun. Brown and I would aim it, Venables would load and fire and Stacey would hand up the clips of ammunition. As predicted, the 88 came back, flying slowly. We laid the gun by sound, and when I judged it to be nearest us, I ordered, "Fire!"

We were all blinded for a moment by the flash of the gun, and the only other result was that the plane instantly accelerated and disappeared. The action was approved by the authorities, though we were warned not to fire from any position which might give away an important target to the enemy.

Our return to the railhead was welcomed. We were not close enough to visit our railway engineers, but our new gun-site was in a huge patch of sweet-scented flowers. An interesting relic nearby was an unexploded 15-inch shell from the battleship H.M.S. *Barham.*

A *khamseen,* or sandstorm, occurred while we were there. *Khamseen* is from the Arabic word for five - *khamsa* - and such storms often blow for five days. The sand finds its way into mouth, nose, eyes and ears. When you finish drinking your tea, there is an inch of the stuff in your mug. In the morning you wake up half-covered with it. We discovered on the third day of the storm a crack in the gun-carriage that needed repair. As no enemy

80

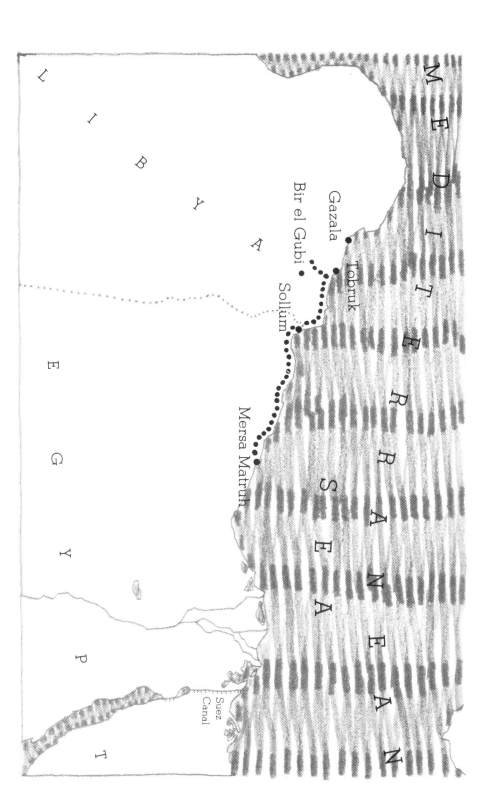

action was possible, I decided to go to Troop Headquarters to report it. The distance was about a mile and I knew the bearing. It was necessary to cover the exposed parts of the body against the scouring effect of sand on skin, so, despite the heat, extra clothing had to be worn. I tried to find the headquarters, but, though I cast around carefully after covering the two thousand paces which I had reckoned to be about a mile, I failed to find it. I had some difficulty on the way back, though I had my compass and an approximate bearing, the gun-site proving elusive in the "couldn't-see-your-hand-in-front-of-your-face" visibility.

Before we left this site, we had to go to the railhead close by to help move some of the loaded freight cars. Here we met Alan Bellamy with some of his detachment. With the reorganization into three-gun troops, Bellamy had been transferred, and this was my first meeting with him since leaving Matruh. The work was not heavy and we had a long chat and parted with a casual farewell. Next day we began our march to the assembly area for the coming battle.

I always liked to know where everything and everybody relevant to the situation were located. A truck with our regiment's markings drew up by the gun and the officer in the front seat called me over and asked me the position of one of the tank units in our brigade. My directions were a model of clarity and accuracy. The officer then proceeded to take me to task for not demanding to see his identity card before telling him anything. He said it was a severe breach of security. My gun detachment enjoyed my discomfort, although I thought the strictures too severe as I knew the sergeant who was sitting with the security officer. The sergeant might have mentioned it!

That the fighting would soon be resumed was obvious. Our forces were holding a defensive position from Gazala, some thirty miles west of Tobruk on the coast, to Bir Hacheim, about thirty miles nearly due south. Extensive mine-fields had been laid. Before moving to our final position, we had a visit from the commander of our brigade. Brigadier Briggs came around inspecting not the usual whitewash, but the morale. When he arrived at our gun, I called the detachment to attention and saluted. He said, "Stand them at ease."

Then he asked casually where our slit trenches were.

"We don't dig slit trenches for gun teams," I said bluntly, without the customary "sir." He seemed pleased, said "Carry on", and I saluted him.

Next day Lt. Mackie, beaming widely, came to see us. "So you had words with the Brigadier," the troop commander said. "He's going around telling everybody how a sergeant told him off! He enjoyed it."

About the same time, another detachment had a less pleasant encounter with the divisional commander. One of the gunners had painted a portrait of the general on the gun, cartoon-style, and had entitled it "General Balls-up", a reference to our first advance and our headlong retreat. The battery commander, the adjutant and the troop commander were with the general, who was, like Queen Victoria, not amused. The officers and the gun detachment were lined up in front of the offending gun. The general then went down the line, naming each in turn: "Major Balls-up, Captain Balls-up, Lieutenant Balls-up, Sergeant Balls-up, Bombarbier Balls-up, Gunner Balls-up..." down to the last gunner!

A few days later we moved for the last time before the battle began. It was just three days after my thirtieth birthday.

CHAPTER 13

KNIGHTSBRIDGE STRAIGHT AHEAD!

The young fell short of glory in the sand.

Sidney Keyes

Rommel attacked the Gazala Line by sending his 15th and 21st Panzer Division and the 90th Panzer Grenadier Division round the south end of the Allied defences, where the Free French forces held Bir Hacheim. The Germans set out in the late evening of May 24th and turned on the Free French and the Seventh Armoured Division just after dawn. After some chaotic fighting, the attack failed and thereafter the battle was mainly fought around Sidi Muftah, known to us as "Knightsbridge." The two armies fought for nearly a month in this comparatively small area.

The morning of May 26th 1942 was unusual. Gunfire was heard in the distance and then some solid tank shells came skipping and bouncing through our formation, so slowly that they were clearly spent, and seemed harmless, almost as if you could field them and throw them back to the wicket-keeper. Lt. Mackie came to warn us to be ready for an imminent move as German armour was headed our way. Hardly had he left when the orders were given.

At that time we were just south of the El Adem Airfield, which was some fifteen miles from Tobruk, but too close to the battle front to be used by the R.A.F. We moved eastward across the south edge of it, and as we did, a Junkers 110 screamed over us about twenty feet up. A moment later there was a sudden un-signalled halt of all vehicles. A German six-wheeled armoured car, driving north towards Tobruk, appeared some two hundred yards in front of us. Its crew realized suddenly that they were not among friends, turned around and fled before anybody thought to do anything, even retreat. The battle had only just started when our battery suffered its first casualty. During the night a

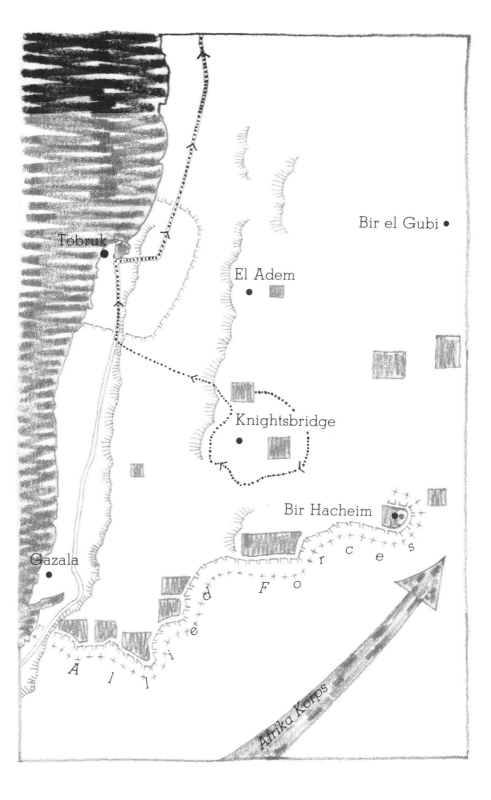

Bir el Gubi •

Tobruk •

El Adem •

Knightsbridge •

Bir Hacheim •

Gazala •

Allied Forces

Afrika Korps

driver with Battery Headquarters was run over by one of our own trucks as he slept. He was injured but not seriously.

Our next move took us to a rocky area. It was customary for us not to wear our shirts when there was likelihood of being wounded, be it by bomb splinter, shell or bullet. Fabric from a garment might be carried deeply into a flesh wound and infection could result. We wore normally, therefore, shorts, stockings, boots and ankle puttees. We were supposed to wear pith helmets or caps. Howson had discarded his shirt and left it on the rocks. When he put it on before preparing a meal, the scorpion which had crawled into the shirt stung him. He yelled, and Brown and I went to his help. We tried to take his shirt off, keeping the scorpion in the folds, but it was able to sting him once more. This badly upset Howson, and I hurried over with him to the ambulance, where a medical orderly casually dabbed iodine on the stings. There were no ill effects.

Scorpions were common, especially in rocky areas. They crawled into boots or beds at night and we jumped quickly out of suspected blankets and shook them out. Boots were never put on carelessly.

Next day, still in the same place, we were surprised to see a Church Army canteen truck come up and open for business. While Bombardier Cooper took over, I went across and bought some tins of pineapple for the detachment. As I came back, a single German plane, taking advantage of a heat haze which hampered observation, bombed us. The concussion of the nearest bomb knocked me down and the tins went flying. I was somewhat bruised and grazed about the hands and knees.

Before we could even open the tins of fruit, nine Stukas came screaming down. One seemed to be diving right at us and it was a frightening eternity before it turned away. One of our shells had hit it on the wing close to the fuselage and it flew off trailing smoke. We reported the hit, our first, and our first daylight action.

While the airplanes we saw most often were the JU 87s, the Stuka dive-bombers, we much preferred the Douglas "Boston" bombers flown by the South African Air Force! They flew over us in tight formation and seconds later we could hear the rumble of their bombs. We always counted them as they came back and never did fewer return than went out during the campaign.

Most of our time during the battle was spent at the gun, instantly ready to engage hostile aircraft. One morning an artillery officer, a major, came to us and asked abruptly why we hadn't a spotter standing and constantly sweeping the sky with field glasses. I said that we hadn't such equipment, but we did have a gunner with very good hearing, and we were ready to fire at any target even before we saw it. He said our orders were to have a spotter, glasses or no glasses. He went off, a doubting Thomas. Shortly afterwards Gunner Stacey alerted us and swung the gun to point at an oncoming plane. We recognized it as soon as it came into sight, a lone Messerschmidt 109 fighter, on reconnaissance. When our sights were laid on it, and the aircraft came within range, we fired. The first shell was so close that the pilot tried a tight turn, but we followed him and he put his plane into a shallow dive to escape at top speed. The officer who had earlier reprimanded us had seen the engagement and came over to congratulate us warmly on the accuracy of our shooting.

We moved the next day and were joined by the support echelon of the Fourth Hussars, Winston Churchill's old regiment. They had obviously had warning of a visit from the great man as they were in a high state of "spit-and-polish." Somebody else knew of their presence, for shortly after their arrival we were heavily bombed. From one of the bombs a small splinter hit me. My shorts were partly unbuttoned for greater coolness and the fragment landed just below my navel. I called out, "I'm hit!"

Perhaps my cry was somewhat theatrical, because the detachment all laughed. I clapped my hand to the damage, too frightened to look. The fragment had struck on its flat side and my only injury, barely visible at that, was a small burn.

The Hussars lost one of their trucks which was loaded with ammunition. It caught fire and for several hours the shells and bullets were exploding. There was no water to spare to put out a fire and the truck had to be left to burn.

Gunners Alf Day and Bill Curtis had joined the Army on the same day and had served together ever since, inseparable. During the raid in which I was almost injured, both were cut down by a bomb. Alf's wound was to the left upper arm and chest, a gaping hole which bled profusely. Bill Curtis had been hit in the leg and had subsided against the gun in a sitting position.

"Look after Alf, I'm all right," he called out.

An ambulance arrived quickly and they were both taken away to a field hospital. Next day we were informed that Bill was dead. All thought that the names had been mixed up, and that Alf had died. A chaplain went to find out the truth. Bill Curtis had quietly bled to death by the time the ambulance had reached the dressing station; Alf was recovering.

Another gunner was added; Parker, who had been driving a Battery three-ton truck. He was young and apparently had not been on good terms with his N.C.O.s. Lt. Mackie had to find a place for him but did not have a driver's job vacant. Parker was willing to learn to serve the gun and began his apprenticeship. We were experimenting at this time with lowering the gun, to improve its stability and the better to conceal it. While we were doing this Parker was smoothing the base of the hole into which a pad was to rest, when the gun tipped and the pad scraped the skin and tissue from the back of his hand from wrist to knuckles. He cried out from pain and shock, near fainting. I walked him over to the ambulance in our formation where the medical attendants took over. I was sorry to lose him, because in a short time he had showed willing and seemed happy in his new role.

The battle was being fought fiercely and, despite the new Grant tank, some of which the armoured brigades had - although not enough - the Germans were gradually winning the slugging match and wearing down our armour. To support the tanks, a battery of 5.5-inch guns was brought up; their longer range and hefty projectiles - heavier than those fired from the twenty-five pounders - made them more effective. They were less mobile and therefore needed to be used with caution in the forward areas.

Lt. Mackie told us we were to protect the new guns from air attack, so we prepared for the move. We found them in a shallow valley, their crews already digging in. As we had not been given our orders before setting out, we had halted, waiting to be told our positions. Immediately a formation of Junkers 88 bombers - twenty-four of them in a compact square - bombed us, all planes releasing their loads simultaneously. They must have found out about the new 5.5-inch guns; perhaps a reconnaissance plane had spotted them, or even an errant armoured car. All we could do was dive for cover. I was terrified; I flung myself head first under a scrub bush, where sand had collected, and clawed myself into the sand. Stacey landed alongside. He saw my terror and said, "Steady, Sarge. I can't stand it if you can't."

The ground heaved and shook with the concussion of the densely grouped explosions and the whole area was showered with bomb splinters as well as rocks and gravel.

My terror was compounded by anger at the thoughtless way we had been directed to the guns before any plan had been made. Before our move, we should have been ordered to spread out, and bring our guns into readiness not nearer than a half mile from the 5.5s.

My complaint about our vulnerability during the bombing did not fall on deaf ears. Our troop commander agreed with me, then took me aside.

"Sergeant, what do you do with Walker when you are in action?"

Before I could answer, he went on to tell me that he had been near a slit trench when the attack began, and had dived in. Walker, a large, heavy man, had followed right on top. After the bombing, Lt. Mackie said, he had had the greatest difficulty disentangling himself from Walker, who was in such a state of abject terror that he was unable to stand for some minutes. I explained that I knew Walker's problem and that I had asked him to stay with and to help Howson the cook and Mason the driver, who were not required on the gun team during the day.

The 5.5s soon moved out, as their presence was known to the enemy. Our orders were to return to the rear echelon of the 2nd Armoured Brigade, our steady job. However, darkness fell before we could find them and it wasn't until next morning, after a breakfastless early move, that we arrived and prepared for action. The prevailing mood was grim as the battle was not going well. We had also missed our day's rations of food, water, petrol and ammunition.

Stacey was the first to alert us.

"A lot of them coming this way," he said.

There were - twenty-four of them - JU 87s. At the moment they came within range, one of "D" Troop's guns was dismantled for maintenance, while the other jammed with the first round, putting it out of action. We were the only gun ready to engage! In close formation, the planes made an ideal target as they flew steadily on, taking no evasive action. Suddenly three of the bombers broke off and dived towards us. We continued to shoot at the main body until they were out of range. Afterwards we counted a dozen bomb splinters around the gun, a legacy from the three 87s which had bombed us. Luckily we had no casualties.

Harry Nayland, the troop sergeant, a World War One veteran, came shortly afterwards with the news that, because of our wandering about the night before, he had missed the ration delivery. However, he had brought along some tea, sugar, milk, biscuits and tins of "bully beef." When he had handed this to the cook, and while the rest of the detachment were picking up the shell cases and preparing more ammunition, Harry said very quietly to me, "A very gallant gentleman died yesterday."

I didn't understand for a moment, despite the obvious effect on him, of what he was telling me. Seeing my bewilderment and realizing that I did not already know his news, and that he had to break it to me, he said simply, "Alan."

"A" Troop had been surprised by the enemy much as we had, and my friend Alan Bellamy and Gunner Mellors had been killed as they tried to bring their gun into action. Gunner Higgins, the driver, was also killed as he leapt from the tow-er, the bomb falling between the truck and the gun.

There was no time to mourn. In wartime death is different; it seems inevitable that friends will die, and when it happens you must get on with the job.

Our supplies arrived next day, including rations for the day we had missed. More important, Harry Nayland told me that the battery sergeant-major had witnessed our engagement with the twenty-four dive-bombers, had counted at least seven hits, and admitted there may have been many more. No other gun had taken part in the action.

A few days of mild sandstorms gave us a slight respite. We moved several more times as the battle swayed to and fro, and during these extremely hot days we again had trouble with the tow-er's engine boiling up. But one day, though the engine seemed very hot, we did not experience our familiar problem.

"Mason, why haven't we boiled up yet?" I asked.

"I've found out how to cure it," said Mason. "I just don't put in so much water."

We stopped - in time to prevent the engine from seizing!

A brigade from an Indian division moved up one hot, sandy day to make a counter-attack, after the enemy had captured one of our defensive positions south of Knightsbridge. Some minutes later a command car containing a general stopped by the gun and called me over. I hurried to the vehicle, followed by the detachment's shouted advice, "Ask for his card, Sarge."

As though he had heard, the polite, white-moustached general said, "You'll need to see this first, Sergeant," and showed me his identity card. He then asked about the Indian units - at what time had they passed through, and in what direction.

Later that day we were warned to prepare at once for a move. We did so and then waited, equipment packed, gun attached to the tow-er. While we were thus idling, a Messerschmidt 109 passed very low overhead, a sitting duck which we would have been unsporting enough to shoot down. In frustration, Walter Brown grabbed a rifle and fired shot after shot at it. As soon as Lt. Mackie showed up, I told him I had talked matters over with the detachment and we wanted to stay in action until the others moved off. We were tired of being caught unprepared by the enemy. I had no need to remind him of the earlier episode with the 5.5 battery. This he agreed to, and thereafter this became our practice, and when we arrived at our general destination, we moved away from the formation and actually went into action while waiting for orders about where to set up.

The next time we were in action, we suffered another misfortune; our gun misfired as we shot at the usual dive-bombers. The Drill Book orders that the gun be re-cocked and fired. If still without success, the shell is to be left for at least one minute before it is unloaded.

"Fire again," I ordered Venables.

He did so. Nothing. In the middle of an air-raid, I thought, none of us wishes to sit on the gun for one minute.

"Unload," I said.

Instantly Stacey, who had guessed what I would order, took the shell as it was ejected, carried it a few yards to our rear, and put it gently into a handy slit trench. We resumed firing for a few seconds until the bombers were out of range. Discussing it later, it was agreed that all concerned would prefer to risk the misfire exploding when unloading rather than wait one minute inactively. Stacey was the one who took the risk, and he said very emphatically, "Unload 'em. I'll take 'em."

We were again in action a few minutes later, and to our surprise an officer from Battery Headquarters had arrived. As we opened fire, he jumped into a nearby slit trench. When the action was over, I walked over to him and saluted. After an exchange of greetings and news of the other troops - "A" "B" and "C" - I pointed out the potential risk from the misfire he had shared the trench with.

Only once did we see a "dog fight" over the desert, and that was a sad sight - three of our planes were shot down quickly and the others dived for home. Until they did, we were unable to intervene, but claimed a hit on one of the Messerschmidt 109s as it turned back towards its lines.

CHAPTER 14

A RETREAT - WITH SIDE-TRIPS

He who lives and runs away, lives to fight another day.

Author unknown

It had become clear by the middle of June that the Eighth Army was weakening and that the battle was lost. Rommel was using his dive-bombers elsewhere for we had not seen any for several days. One day we had stopped near a battery of 25-pound field guns. While we watched, two single shells from the enemy landed some four or five hundred yards away to one side of the 25-pounders. Bombardier Cooper, a regular artilleryman, said the Germans were ranging in on the British battery without alarming them into moving. Within a minute salvo after salvo crashed down. The field-gunners went to ground in their slit trenches, and after a five minute pounding emerged apparently unscathed.

We suffered a few very bad moments when an enemy self-propelled gun, much like a tank without a turret, fired airbursts over us of shrapnel shells which were timed to explode some fifty feet overhead. The gun was out of sight and we could do nothing to silence it.

Our worsening plight told on some of the detachment. We were mixed up on the fringe of the fierce ground fighting, and Mason drove us down a steep slope to within six inches of a rock face where a large truck or tank had dug in to gain some shelter from shellfire. He was shaking and I asked Walter Brown to take over. Walter was a skillful driver, imperturbable as the Sphinx. As he was also indispensible on the gun, I had not wanted him to drive except in extreme need.

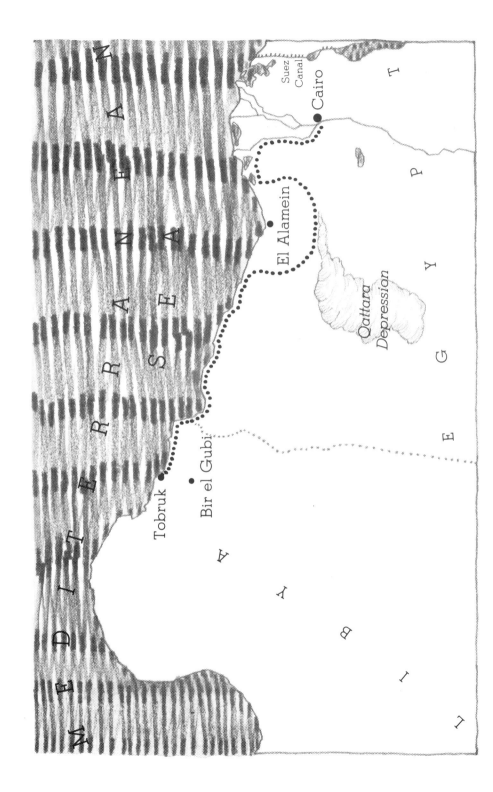

That evening we were outside the western perimeter of the Tobruk defences and were ordered to be ready to move. We had our evening meal and made an extra brew of tea to carry in our large vacuum container.

We were instructed to put a large white cloth over the gun muzzle, as we were to travel as close together in a single column as we could. We moved about eleven p.m. and bumped slowly north until we met the coast road. Here we turned east, which meant we were going into Tobruk. The possibility of being besieged there worried me. There was a by-pass which passed south of Tobruk, connecting the coast road west and east of the town. It was more than likely, however, that the Germans would have cut it off by now. Our next hazard was a bridge over a wide wadi which was being shelled by a single enemy gun, probably with indirect and unobserved fire. As the column reached the bridge it halted, and each vehicle in turn raced across. Before we had to, I saw several shells, about forty-five seconds apart, fall near without hitting bridge, road or vehicle. Brown sped us across safely between shells, and we were soon through Tobruk and about five miles beyond. All night as we travelled east, I watched the Plough turn around the Pole Star. As dawn broke, we stopped, dispersed.

We had been warned that Arabs had been seen in the battle area and it was thought that some of them were acting as agents for the enemy. We were told to detain them. Just as Howson was preparing breakfast, an Arab came to us with eggs to sell. Acting on information received, we proceeded to the scene of the crime, arrested the suspect and took him into custody. Two gunners escorted him to Lt. Mackie's truck. We also arrested and detained his eggs, but they did not reach the higher authorities. They were very small, and each of the detachment had three, fried with our bacon.

Our retreat continued until we passed through the border wire, still on the coast road. We were given a position very close to the frontier on the Egyptian side. It was most unpleasant because of the stench of decay and the many flies. When the cook dug a hole to bury rubbish, he came across a body a mere eighteen inches below the surface! Wherever we dug, it was the same. We moved away from this malodorous place to a pleasant site among some scrub. There we slept well after a disturbed night the day before.

Lt. Mackie came early next morning with his worried look very obvious. He found it extremely hard to pass on orders such as he now brought us. He had been told to place a gun on the Libyan side of the wire to challenge anything that came down the road. Tobruk had fallen and we could expect the enemy any time now. Very apologetically, Lt. Mackie said, "Sergeant, don't wait for orders or hesitate to come back inside the wire if you think it's too dangerous."

We packed up and went through a gap in the hundred yard belt of barbed wire. Close to this gap was a slight rise where we could command a good view of any vehicle heading for the opening. The detachment was not pleased with this assignment, the defence of one of the gaps in the wire by a single 40 mm. gun firing a 2-pound shell. However, nothing happened for the first two hours of our vigil.

Suddenly, dust on the horizon warned us of an approaching vehicle, coming towards us so fast that it was too late to retreat inside the fence. We laid the gun on it and followed the target, ready to fire. It was a three-ton truck, one of ours - unless, of course, it had been captured. When it reached us it stopped. I went over to talk to the driver, but he jumped out of the cab without saying a word and went to the back, climbing over the tailgate. I was near enough to see that his head was bandaged and that the bandage was blood-stained. He appeared at the rear of the truck and said, "Catch, mate."

I held out both arms and he dropped a large shallow box into them. Without another word, he ran back to the cab and drove off through the wire at great speed. I took the box over to the gun and opened it. There were two dozen cans of American beer, two each all round! The beer was hot, and, on opening, shot high into the air. There was more foam than beer. Brown and I dug a hole and buried our cans, with good results when we drank them later.

The troop commander came in the late afternoon, looking much happier. We were to come inside the wire and the Engineers were going to close the gap and plant mines. I gave him a can of beer and told him how we came to have them.

We had a quiet night again and heard that each of the three detachments in "D" Troop were to have a day off duty, in turn, down the escarpment on the sands near Sollum. We were to go on the morrow. Sergeant Addy's gun had already left.

Next morning, we drove down the precipitous road from the escarpment to the coastal plain and found a suitable place to swim. The water was warm but salty and stimulating. An order from Battery Headquarters reached us in the afternoon. The retreat was to continue - our destination, Mersa Matruh. We were to be ready to fall in the line of march behind the rest of "D" Troop as they moved past us, after dark. So the rest of the day we spent swimming and sun-bathing.

Walter Brown and I took the gun tow-er to a petrol point to fill up the tank and our empty containers from the last ration delivery. A water truck was giving water out and we filled some four-gallon containers that we had received from the South African Engineers. We were about to return when we were told that the food dump was open to all before being destroyed to deny it to the enemy. We found it and went in. The demolitions were being set but we were able to load cases of tinned fruit, bacon, tomatoes, carrots and potatoes as well as several thousand cigarettes and cases of Army biscuits. We returned, hitched up the gun and waited to join the column.

Our journey to Mersa Matruh was uneventful. The Battery took up position on the western side of the town, north of the coast road. We were in a rather exposed position, in front of one wadi and with another some hundred yards behind us. We had only seen one airplane since arriving two days earlier. It was near midnight when a large plane cruised around, showing no lights. We had been warned that friendly aircraft would stay out of the area so that we thought it was hostile. The short burst we fired narrowly missed, and startled it into turning on lights which plainly revealed the large red cross of an ambulance plane. No damage was done.

The ground was very rocky and on the afternoon of the second day we became the target of a small calibre enemy field-gun. We had difficulty in digging slit trenches and those we did make were shallow. I had the gun tow-er taken into the wadi to our rear where it was quite safe. The sniping continued and, though the shells seemed ineffective, I walked over to Troop Headquarters and asked for permission to find a less vulnerable gun-site. As soon as the gun was out of action, the tow-er came up and we found a good place in a wadi which gave us protection and a good field of fire.

Troop Headquarters was the victim the next day of an attack by a single R.A.F. Hurricane fighter. Flying up the wadi only a few feet above the ground, the plane's eight machine-guns destroyed a three-ton truck and put five bullets through the calf muscle of Lt. Mackie's driver, miraculously missing the bone. The stores and equipment in the truck were torn to ribbons and the chassis had many holes drilled in it. It was fortunate that the troop commander and his 15-hundredweight truck were elsewhere.

Lance-Bombardier Fletcher had been complaining of stomach pains, diagnosed by me as "gippy tummy" or colitis. He thought it was worse than this, and wanted to report sick. Therefore, when Sergeant Nayland left after delivering our rations, he took Fletcher with him, to be passed on to the nearest medical aid post. We all realized at this time that the fighting had moved past Matruh and it was no surprise when we were told to be ready to move out that night. As was now our custom, we kept the gun in action while having everything else packed away after we had eaten an early evening meal.

As the sun was dipping to the western horizon, we heard and almost immediately saw an Italian biplane, a contemporary of our Gloucester Gladiator, dating from the nineteen-thirties. It was at extreme range but we were able to fire one long burst at it. To our disappointment it seemed we had missed, but the biplane went into a long shallow dive and disappeared from sight. Some days later, at our next contact with our battery headquarters, we learned that our first shell had hit the propeller centre, the spinner, causing the airplane to crash, and that no other gun had engaged it.

We were led on to the coast road about nine p.m. This time we had no difficulty in seeing ahead as the night was clear and moonlit. Our orders were to follow closely the vehicle ahead, as the first few miles were through a minefield. There was a long delay while we were formed up on the road, during which a R.A.F. Wellington bomber cruised back and forth machine-gunning the column! We could do nothing about it, but finally the plane desisted. Almost at once we moved forward and turned south from the coast road into the minefields.

Progress was slow and Brown drove carefully in the tracks of the gun in front of us, mindful of the warning. We were surprised, therefore, to see one of our trucks leave the column and pull out some twenty yards to the right. Even as I opened my mouth to mention it, the truck detonated a mine and came to a stop. We were relieved to see the driver and his mate jump from it and run over to the column, apparently unhurt. The truck was abandoned.

The column halted a little later; the guns were having difficulty crossing the railway. We solved it by approaching at a very slight angle and then easing each wheel of the gun-carriage in turn over the two rails. This entailed four lifts over each rail, eight in all. By the time we had done this, the rest of the column was out of sight and we realized that we were now the rear vehicle.

A glance at the stars gave me the direction - due south. The previous vehicles had left no visible wheel marks on the surface, so we used dead reckoning. Not long after this Walter Brown said, conversationally, "Look over here - this side."

I did so. There was a German armoured car, against which a sentry leaned, a Schmeisser automatic gun on his arm! He saw us, took a step forward, but then relaxed and leaned back again. By this time I had looked out on my side, and I said, "Now look out this way."

About fifty enemy trucks were drawn up in close laager, with five or six men sleeping alongside each! Finally, Brown solved our problem. "Let's look straight ahead," he suggested.

Probably the German sentry, unfamiliar with our equipment, had thought we were Italians, especially as we were four days behind the main German advance.

That we were so far to the rear of the fighting was brought home to us even more dramatically a few minutes later when we crossed a landing-field where JU 87s and 88s were dispersed. We saw no sentries, tents or vehicles but deemed it expedient to press on. It was lucky we did, for we had only put two or three miles behind us when a front gun-carriage wheel punctured.

As we had no spare wheel, and because it would be difficult if not impossible to tow the gun, we decided we would take the gun off the carriage as we did when putting it in action, and then secure it to the rear of the tow-er and pull it on the rear wheels only. We were about to do this when our troop commander came, a shepherd looking for the long lost sheep. He vetoed our idea and told us to wait while he went for a spare wheel. Meanwhile we took off the punctured one, and Lt. Mackie returned quickly with the spare. He told us the track up the escarpment was not far away, straight ahead, and that he would wait for us at the top.

I was appalled at the first sight of the track up the escarpment. It looked impossibly steep and already some trucks and a 25-pounder had been abandoned where they had toppled. As we started up the slope, I moved from my seat in the cab to sit on the step leading into the cab whence I could leap clear if the tow-er toppled. Brown laughed at my fear.

"No difficulty taking this up," he said, "but I'll have to drop into low gear in four-wheel drive."

"Can we stop on this slope to do that?" I asked, since normally a change into four-wheel drive needs the vehicle at rest. He laughed again and, as we crawled up, changed into four-wheel drive without a hitch. We reached the top safely and drew up behind one of our guns. It was near dawn and before first light a phenomenon occurred which I had not seen before in the desert, nor did I ever see again; a dense mist settled over the area and shrouded us from view.

I waited for several minutes in the cab of the truck, expecting the column to move. As nothing happened I went forward to the next gun and found driver and sergeant asleep. While they had slept, the vehicles in front had moved off, leaving us lost in the mist!

"Which way do we go?" the rudely-awakened sergeant asked.

"Go straight ahead; we'll see the others when the mist clears," I advised.

So it proved, and an hour later we caught up with the rest of the column. Lt. Mackie came alongside in his truck and told us that we'd better keep going before stopping for breakfast.

About nine o'clock we paused for a welcome mug of tea with bacon and tomatoes from our Sollum loot. We had just resumed our march when a Messerschmidt 110, the German twin-engine fighter, flew low over us. The direction of the column was still due south and, expecting that the plane identified us, Lt. Mackie changed the direction to southeast. There was no cover in the desert, but probably the Luftwaffe had bigger targets to attack, and anyway, we were well behind the German ground forces.

The war was suspended for a few minutes for the next incident. A cloud of dust heralded a vehicle, travelling north towards the German forces. Our column stopped, but the approaching truck did not slacken speed nor turn to left or right. As it sped through we could see that it was chasing a gazelle. In the truck were two British soldiers - a driver and a passenger, who was leaning forward, firing a revolver at the gazelle, and shouting "Tally-ho!"

This was the hottest day we had experienced in the desert. It was very flat, and therefore the usual mirage of a wide expanse of water was constantly seen. Next we saw the second most common mirage; the trucks looked elongated, seeming like a fleet of yachts with sandy sails. Such a fleet came towards us. Our concern was, were they friend or foe? Our troop commander asked me if I could identify the formation, and I said, thinking of boats, "Shall I put a shot across their bows?"

He said no, and set off on his truck to find out while we waited. It turned out to be a small fighting patrol harassing the enemy supply trucks. The commander advised Lt. Mackie to go south to the edge of the salt marshes, known as the Qattara Depression, and follow it eastwards until we reached our own lines.

We stopped for a meal near sunset and for a check on supplies: food, water and petrol. Every vehicle reported that all was well. After the meal, I walked a few yards away from the gun and saw a large black bird. Its wings were clipped and though it could not fly, neither could it be caught. Between its flutters it was croaking hoarsely, "Heil Hitler!" The raven was probably a casualty of the rapid German advance into Egypt.

We had reached the Qattara Depression and were keeping close to it next day. It was quiet, yet very hot. During the afternoon we were bombed by our own planes, the Bostons that we had so carefully counted as they came back from raids. Their mistake was excusable since we were still on the wrong side of the lines. The whine of their bombs falling was a shock, as we had seen them seconds before without thinking that all they could see was a column of guns - undoubtedly German - moving towards the Alamein defences, that were being desperately prepared. The single column of widely-spaced guns made a poor target and there were no casualties.

Later that day Lt. Mackie's driver drove the truck into an innocuous looking patch of scrub and became stuck fast in sand. As we came up to the area, Walter Brown, who was driving, said, "Let's pull him out."

We unhitched the gun and drove into the sand, using the four-wheel drive. Lt. Mackie waved his long arms furiously to stop us, shouting, "Go back! Don't risk it."

Without taking any notice, Brown swung the tractor around and backed up to the truck. We secured it with the tow-er's winch-rope and pulled the truck out to firm ground.

That night it was decided to keep going. Very little fighting or movement normally took place during the hours of darkness and it was hoped that safety could be reached soon after dawn. After a cold and uneventful night march, we passed through our own lines at the southern end of the Alamein defences. Already Rommel was attacking at the other end, near the coast.

We were in Cairo later that day. Although our wanderings made us the last to arrive, we had experienced the best of the retreat. Most of the Battery, including the headquarters, had suffered shelling and machine-gunning as they ran the gauntlet of an enemy attack, leaving Matruh on the east side. For us, the longest way round had been the safest way home.

CHAPTER 15

PICKING UP THE PIECES

Theirs not to make reply,
Theirs not to reason why,
Theirs but to do and die.

Alfred, Lord Tennyson

The Battery had sustained casualties in the retreat. The head-quarters and half the gun detachments had been on the east side of Matruh. Their break-out had been through the battle line between the Afrika Corps and the New Zealand Division, which had come up to help stem the German advance. Gunner Black, with whom I had joined the Battery, was killed by machine-gun fire as he jumped on the gun to load it. Lance-Bombardier Fletcher, whom we had tried to keep with us, was believed prisoner with many others who had not answered roll-call after the night of the break-out.

Walter Brown and I were paraded before the colonel of the regiment to be told that he was approving our applications for commissions and that we would hear when we were to appear before the Selection Board.

All our guns and vehicles were handed in and we were sent to Alexandria. There we were to be given jobs while we waited for reinforcements to return us to full strength. I was sent to Mustapha Barracks to take charge of the guard at the main entrance. The guard's responsibility was to see that all who entered had either a pass or a movement order authorizing them to enter the camp. The civilian workers were checked going out to make sure they had no stolen goods. It was boring. The main diversions were the chameleon, the pet of the guard-room, and the corporal in charge of the Army bakery.

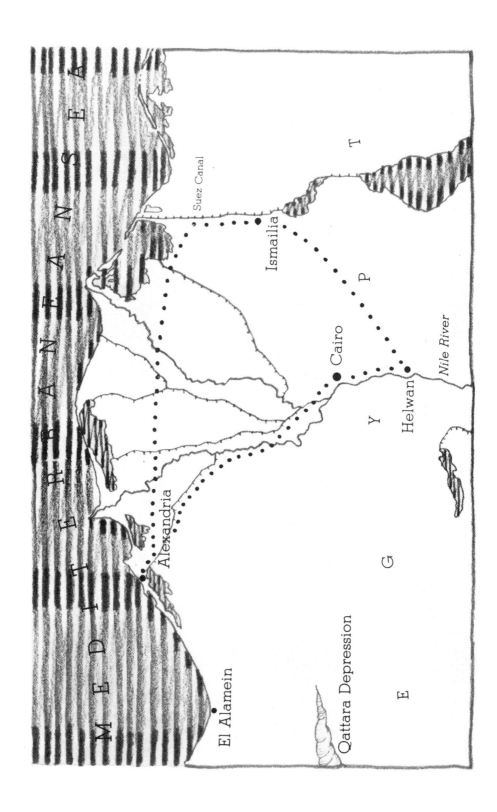

MEDITERRANEAN SEA

Suez Canal

Ismailia

T

Cairo

P

Helwan

Nile River

Y

Alexandria

G

El Alamein

E

Qattara Depression

The chameleon kept the insects down; it was tame, and would sit on your hand. Everybody liked the chameleon. The Corporal-baker would sit beside you when he visited the guard-room each evening, and put his hand on your knee. He was a homosexual, and nobody liked him. Gunner Searchfield, one of the guards and the Battery humorist, found out that the Corporal was a valuable source of cakes, which were baked every evening. Searchfield took his virtue into jeopardy each night and, with devious half-promises, returned intact with a large bag of cakes for the guard. The baker began to require more than promises and Searchfield became reluctant to run the risk. Before a crisis was reached, we were suddenly taken off the guard duty. I was now assigned to be in charge of the detention cells in the Barracks.

This was not an enviable position. The cells held prisoners awaiting courts-martial, as well as those who had committed petty offences and were awaiting transport to take them back to their units. These latter were usually in the cells only overnight. There were no standing orders or instructions extant, and the guards were as unfamiliar with the job as I was, nor did any officer ever inspect the cells. We were left alone to carry out the responsibilities.

The first difficulty encountered was a prisoner awaiting court-martial who was an escape artist of considerable talent. Ordinary handcuffs and leg-irons he opened with ease, yet he was required to be so restrained at all times. The Military Police lent me a very special pair of handcuffs with which the wrists are held one on top of the other, almost as if the prisoner has his arms folded in front of him. Unfortunately the prisoner's wrists were too thick for even the largest pair of this type.

One night the Military Police brought in an Australian on leave who was fighting drunk. It required the two "Red-caps" and two of the guards to subdue him and put him in the cells. We asked for, and were given, two large good-natured judo experts to act - not as "chuckers-out" but as "chuckers-in." They were soon in action. Another Australian was brought in and refused to go into the cells.

"No Pommie bastard will make me," he boasted. The guard woke me and I carefully put my sergeant's stripes on my arm.

Then I walked up to the Australian and said, "I'm going to give a proper order. Now, you are under arrest. Go quietly to the cells."

He repeated his earlier assertion and our two strong-arm guards quickly and - as far as I could see - painlessly put him in the cells.

The escape artist came to an agreement about handcuffs. We would handcuff him and he would wait until we left before he took them off. Furthermore, he would put them back on if there was an inspection. Despite this accommodation, we were glad when he went to his court-martial and we saw no more of him.

Some men from one of the Guards' regiments were in the cells. They had fought in the Knightsbridge battle and all the way back to Alamein, without respite. They then became part of the defensive line formed. After a request for leave had been refused, they took a truck and some rations and left their unit, rested for a few days, and then returned. They were awaiting court-martial.

Before we were relieved of our duties, a break-out had been planned but was betrayed by one of the prisoners. Two bars had been sawn through in the washroom and the cuts concealed with soap and dust. With the bars removed, the space would have been enough for a man to squeeze through. The whole place - including prisoners and their possessions - was searched without warning. We found three pieces of hacksaw blade. The bars were replaced, and the balance sheet showed the correct number of prisoners when we marched out with an audible sigh of relief.

Reinforcements had arrived and the Battery gathered in a camp not far from Ismailia. The journey was made by road on a very hot day. Walter Brown and some others decided to swim in the canal by which we had halted. This was strictly forbidden. They were discovered by the Sergeant-Major, who took their names, Bilharzia, or hookworm, is contracted in such waters, and the treatment - nineteen inoculations in the abdominal muscles - is a painful ordeal, punishment enough for Brown and his fellow swimmers.

The camp was flat and featureless. At about three o'clock every afternoon, "dust devils" developed in the area. These were like miniature tornadoes, whirling pillars of sand which moved rapidly on the surface, and caused havoc if they struck a tent, either blowing it down or filling it with a cloud of dust.

In re-forming the Battery, the experienced gunners had to be spread evenly as a nucleus for each detachment. Walter Brown, who had been promoted to lance-bombardier during the battle, now became a sergeant and detachment commander, a late but much deserved recognition of his worth. Bombardier Cooper was also promoted sergeant. Harold Stacey and Doug Venables went elsewhere, a great gain to their new detachment. Brown, Stacey and Venables had made my gun team the best in the Battery and I was lucky to have had them. For a week I was troop sergeant and might have continued as such, had not Sergeant Halton reported to Battery Headquarters and been promptly returned to "D" Troop. As Halton was senior to me, Lt. Mackie told me apologetically (since he had made me troop sergeant), it was better that he should take over while I return to the task of detachment commander. I thought this best, too.

A sports day was held. This was an inter-troop competition, what the Army calls a "Tabloid Sports" in which all take part. "D" Troop won and accepted gratefully the prize, a jar of rum. Many of us drank deeply that Saturday evening. The Church Parade next morning was attended compulsorily by all and we were marched back to camp to find an Army blood bank unit awaiting us. Very quickly our blood was sampled and some of us were asked back to donate our pint. I did not find these ceremonies helpful in curing a hangover. I looked so green that one of the blood bank sergeants noticed it and brought a doctor. He asked for my blood sample, lifted my eyelid and pronounced me one hundred over proof, adding that alcohol with a dash of blood made for a poor transfusion.

We picked up new equipment and were placed on the western side of Alexandria to defend the docks. Our reinforcements now had to be drilled on the guns and made into efficient teams. The most recent arrivals had come directly from the U.K. None of them was A-1 medical category and I had three men who had impediments to full participation: one had a metal plate in his head and was not to stay too long in the sun; another was unable to lift anything but the lightest of burdens because of hernia; a third, owing to bad legs, with no special reason given, could not remain standing for long. On the credit side, Burchill, a Liverpudlian, went some way toward replacing Stacey as far as strength was concerned.

The Army panacea is "spit-and-polish." In battle-dress there isn't anything to polish, but there was plenty of brass on the gun. A colonel of the Royal Marines was area commander and he came around with the battery commander to visit us and watch some gun-drill. We had had some planes flying for us to practise our drill and he asked me, "Do the planes find you for the practices?"

"Yes sir, I think they see the reflection from the brass parts of the gun," I answered.

Some while after the visit, I was called in to Battery Headquarters to be reprimanded for my response. I said I thought the "smartening-up" was necessary, but the brass polishing on the gun was not desirable in an operational role. My views were not readily accepted; apparently I was not in the Army to think.

We moved to the Alexandria Airfield at Lake Mariut. This was interesting, partly for the great variety of new planes which used it, many of which we had not seen at close quarters. The Mitchells, Marauders and Liberators of the U.S. Air Force landed frequently. The other great interest was the mosquito. This insect lived by day in the ridges of our tents in immense numbers, a solid mass a foot wide the whole length of the tent. At dusk they swarmed out while we took refuge in our mosquito nets. Guards on duty had to have their bodies covered, wearing slacks tucked into socks, gloves with long cuffs over shirt sleeves, and a veiled hat.

Here we received our last reinforcement. He arrived with the rations and the cook took care of him. I was talking to Harry Nayland and could hear the new man complaining that he thought he should not have to serve on the gun; he didn't think he was well enough. He seemed on the point of tears. The cook tried to reassure him.

"Tha's coom to the reet place, lad," he said, and then explained that Sergeant Waters would look after him and see him all right. Pearson was the cook, a Yorkshire man who had been a prison warder in Leeds Gaol before the war. He was not loth to reminisce, in fact did so by the hour with the rest of the detachment entranced by this other world. Pearson's tales of condemned murderers, their ghastly crimes, their executions and the other lesser criminals - the rapists, the burglars and confidence-tricksters - were a splendid help to our morale.

Lake Mariut was pleasant despite the mosquitoes and we were sorry to leave it. We went back to the desert, to an airfield that the Boston bombers, the Eighth Army's Air Force co-operation squadron, were using for some training while another squadron of Baltimore planes, a later version of the Boston, were operational. By the kindness of the squadron's South African commanding officer, all of us who wished were taken up for flights. These were exciting, because the South African Air Force fighters, the American-made Tomahawks and Warhawks, were using the Bostons as targets for attack. They came from behind and floated, as it seemed, just over us. From the air I was particularly interested to notice the sharp delineation between the blue sea and the Egyptian delta, its green vegetation and dazzling white buildings framed by the dull grey desert.

All was not paradisiacal, though. A new officer, a Lt. Jackson, had joined the troop. He regaled us with horrific stories of his training before coming overseas. The assault course had included a shallow trench roofed with dense barbed wire through which you had to crawl flat on your stomach. The floor of the trench, before the course was used, was strewn with the entrails of animals obtained from the local slaughter house. Somebody told the officer he thought he'd rather do that in England than stand on the gun in the desert while Stukas screamed down bombing him.

One day Sergeant Nayland came with the rations and told me that Lt. Jackson was going to visit the gun-sites that coming night, and should reach us about midnight. The purpose of the inspection was to test the efficiency of the sentries, who, ideally, should not be seen or heard. We briefed the two sentries most likely to be on guard, one before midnight, the other after, and decided that a side of one of the tents in deep shadow of the moon, then almost full, would be the best place for the sentry. I suggested they noisily rattle the bolts of their weapons as they challenged. All went as planned. Lt. Jackson returned in the morning and told us how well the guard had performed.

"I'm pleased he did well," I said, "but he did forget one thing."

"What was that?" the officer asked.

I then told him there had been many thefts by natives. I had, therefore, ordered that if anyone came into our area the guard should shoot first and challenge later. The detachment who were nearby on the gun found that more amusing than did Lt. Jackson.

I had acquired an iron bedstead and a mattress on our travels. Even with the extra space this took up, our two tents were roomy enough for the detachment. One night, just after the final battle of Alamein, there was a very heavy windstorm. My bedhead was lashed to the tent pole on the windward side. Soon the other tent blew down and its occupants came in to share ours. Three bedded down with me on the bed, and although the wind blew all night, keeping us all awake, the tent held up. As we learned later, it was the only one that did.

We were still in the same place at Christmas. The Battery made a special effort to provide a traditional meal. Even more important, an adequate supply of beer was obtained. Christmas Day was a great success, with credit due to the cooks for making the meal palatable despite the ingredients, as magical a transformation as any Drury Lane pantomime. The beer lasted well into the night. Gunner Cobbett, who had cast some doubt on my abilities before the Knightsbridge battle, and whom I hadn't seen since, came with an outstretched hand and apologized. He said (omitting the extraneous expletives), "I was wrong; yours was the best detachment. I wish I'd been on it."

The following day was the pay-off. Many were the groans and retchings. Gunner Gaunt came to me in obvious distress, but I couldn't understand from his mumblings what his troubles were. At last, by showing a remarkable talent for mime, he managed to explain that sometime during the night's revels he had lost both upper and lower dentures. I spoke to Captain Rogers at headquarters, where we had dined and drunk. He replied to my enquiry at some length.

"Sergeant," he said, "I don't know if or when Gunner Gaunt will get his teeth. We have a great many here. The troop sergeant is sorting them now into full set, single upper set, single lower and partial plates. When this is done, all the teeth will be sent to all the gun-sites and Gaunt can claim his, if he lost them here."

Captain Rogers was said to be an actor by profession. He may well have been, possibly a stand-up comedian. Later that day, Gaunt came to thank me, again able to talk intelligibly.

The desert war was now a long way from Alamein, the most easterly advance of the German and Italian armies. Their retreat was being bitterly fought, but they would be no more threat to Egypt. We now moved to man gun-sites on the Suez Canal near its southern end. The canal was within range of the German bombers in Crete. My gun was placed on a small, very steep hillock on the bank. It was with difficulty that we manoeuvred the gun into place and returned the tractor to the bottom of the hill.

For once, Authority did not persuade us that danger was imminent, but organized some diversions. Driving instruction was given to all detachment commanders and some selected gunners to ensure two competent drivers were available in all detachments. From my experience this was a necessity and it was fortunate for us at Knightsbridge that Walter Brown had been there to take over. On one occasion we amused ourselves briefly by watching the huge Italian battleship *Veneto Vittorio* come through the canal after its surrender. A battery field hockey team was organized on which I played. This gave Pearson, the erstwhile prison warder, now our cook and telephonist, the chance to relay messages from headquarters in broadest Yorkshire.

"Sergeant, tha's laiking hockey while Thursday," he would tell me. Loosely translated, but without the richness of the original, this meant that I was to play hockey on Thursday.

Time was found for some mobile training and, in the absence of our troop commander, I was given command of the troop for one such exercise, a reminder that I was still waiting to be called before the Selection Board for officer training.

The detachment had been adopted by a ten-year-old boy, Mohammed, who spoke some English and seemed to live nearby. He apparently preferred living with us. This required some subterfuge to prevent discovery for him and disaster for me, since it was strictly forbidden to allow civilians on the site at any time. He usually slept in one of our tents, ate breakfast with us and then disappeared until evening when inspections or visits from officers were much less likely. "Fifi", a woolly-coated puppy, joined the detachment and was pampered and grossly over fed. When challenged by the troop commander, I claimed that we kept her because of her ability to keep the rats down, and nothing more was said. A less likely ratter has never been seen.

When we were to leave our site on the Suez Canal, we had the problem of taking the gun out of action and hitching it to the tractor. The gun had a brake on the rear carriage which was worked by a gunner in the rear of the tractor, using a line secured to a toggle on the short rope from the brake. Gunner Burchill said he would stand on the carriage and apply the brake while the rest of us let the gun down holding the trail. Theoretically this was the simplest way to lower the gun from its high position to the base where the tractor stood. Unfortunately Burchill could not, while standing on the carriage, apply the brake sufficiently even to slow down the gun, and the slope was too great for the rest of us to keep on our feet. The gun swooped down the slope, scattering us. Burchill threw himself off and we watched helplessly at the gun running amok, heading straight for the tractor and the battery trucks waiting to load the equipment. At the very bottom of the slope, the trail dug into the ground, the gun slewed, started toward the top again and rolled back to stop right by the tractor, an almost unbelievable modern miracle!

We were now ready for the move, which was to Helwan, a large town some twelve miles south of Cairo. Mohammed and Fifi came with us. Mohammed brought his father to assure me that he had his family's blessing to make the journey. The only interest of this move was that the stepped pyramid of Sakkhara was within sight of our tents. No useful purpose could be found for our being there, and no doubt other batteries were moving round too, while a higher authority determined our fate.

It seemed impossible for us to rejoin the Armoured Division on account of our many low-category gunners. I still wore the divisional sign, the rhinoceros, mainly because we had been told to remove it from our sleeves. Too many, officers included, seemed to hope that we would not return to the Division, since it was far more dangerous than any other Bofors assignment. The only surprise we had in Helwan was that Mohammed received a letter asking him to return home. He was sad to go and cried a little. We too were sorry; we had enjoyed his company.

We stayed only a few days after Mohammed's departure. Heliopolis, the aerodrome for Cairo, was our new site. We were

112

on the perimeter, but much closer to human habitation than was usually the case, in fact too close for comfort. Thieving was rampant, the thieves myriad. At night, our rifles had to be chained to the tent poles of the single large tent which held the whole detachment. The stories told us were usually about India where the thieves stole the sheets from your bed while you slept in them, without waking you. The second night we were in Heliopolis I woke up and realized there were two intruders in the tent. One was carefully lifting Gunner Greenhow by his shoulders off his battle-dress blouse, which he was using as a pillow, while the other was searching the blouse pockets. I shouted and jumped up. They dropped Greenhow and ran empty-handed.

While at Heliopolis I went on seven days leave and took the train to Alexandria where I enjoyed the freedom to come and go as I wished for a week. While I was taking a walk after breakfast, one of the swarms of bootblacks asked to clean my already well-polished boots. I said no. He then threw some mud on them, mud normally used, along with brushes, in the polishing process. He persisted and I again refused. At this point he was joined by another man who stepped up to me and poked a knife, which he had secreted under his ankle-length garment, into my ribs. They wanted my Army paybook, which had a black market value, as well as my money. I did not know what to do, except struggle as slowly as possible to get my paybook out of the buttoned breast-pocket of my shirt. I was in luck. Before I had managed to produce the book, an Egyptian policeman, complete with a short carbine, turned the corner. I gave a shout. "Help!"

My attackers ran, boot polishing box and all.

I had only been back from leave for a few days when Walter Brown and I were taken away in a truck with all our kit to Abbassia Barracks in Cairo, to take the Officers' Selection Board test, a three-day ordeal.

PART SIX
ACRE, 1943

CHAPTER 16

SELECTION OF OFFICERS - AN INEXACT SCIENCE

All authority must be out of a man's self.

Francis Bacon

I arrived at Abbassia Barracks not knowing what to expect, and what did happen was surprising. My own background knowledge was of a candidate who was ushered in to face the Board and was immediately failed because of an inability to answer the first question. "What colour is a piebald horse?"

Obviously he was not fit to be an officer, since any gentleman could have answered such a simple question. I was ready for that one.

The Board which Walter Brown and I faced was a three-day circus in a square ring. It comprised two interviews, the first with a regular officer, an old-fashioned colonel, the second with a psychiatrist - to make sure that our minds were as fit as our bodies for battlefield stress. There were intelligence tests of the usual type and psychological word association tests. Physical tests were for fitness, ability to climb and leadership capability. The candidates were also under scrutiny in the mess tent at meals when the officers of the Staff mingled and chatted very informally.

My first interview went off very well. The dress was drill shirt and shorts, hose-tops, gaiters and boots. My stripes were, as was the custom, of white tape, with the gun, also in tape, sewn above the three stripes. The officer escorting us into the Selection Board did not recognize the gun, taking it for a misshapen crown and therefore announced me as a staff-sergeant. From his rows of medal ribbons, I could tell the colonel had vast experience and

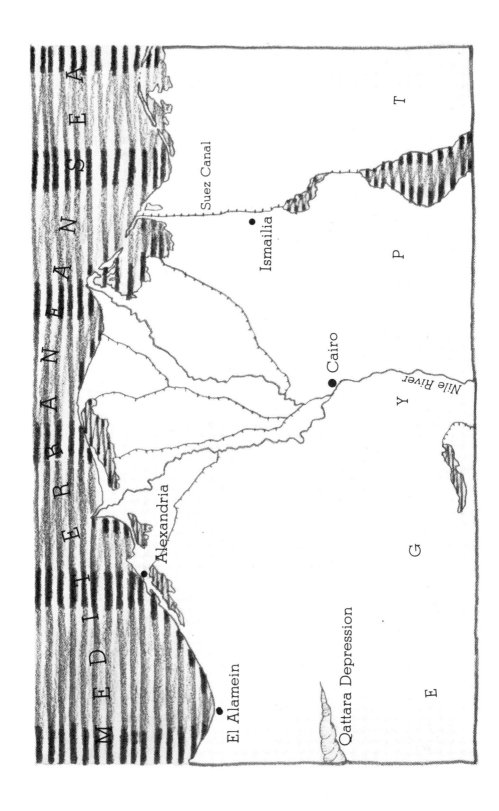

was a regular soldier. He asked me a few questions about my length of service and where I had served. These were pleasant to answer and he nodded approvingly. His next question seemed to me to be the important one.

"You won't make much money if you do become an officer, you know. What is your financial position?"

I answered instantly, "I have no worries at all, sir."

This answer apparently delighted him.

"Very good, very," he said and I was wheeled out after saluting him. I am sure he completely misunderstood my answer, since I merely meant that I was of necessity resigned to living on my pay, whereas he probably thought I meant I had a large fortune.

We were formed into syndicates of six for the physical tests. We climbed up one rope, and at the top were able to reach a second, down which we slid. I surprised myself with the speed I climbed to the top of the first rope and crossed to the other. A game something like a dangerous version of blind-man's-buff was played between two syndicates. A captain was nominated from each and the rest were blindfolded. The object was for the captain to direct his blind troops across the other syndicate's base-line while defending his own ground. This caused some casualties from collisions and head-knockings. My syndicate was successful on the two occasions we played, once when I was captain. The problem we failed was when the whole syndicate had to reach and remain on top of a wooden wall some fourteen feet high. We had a large and heavy man left on the ground. As the smallest and lightest I went down again and, standing on my shoulders, he managed to reach the top with help from the rest. Then someone was lowered head first and I jumped to grasp his hands. Unfortunately, our hands were wet from sweat and I could not hold long enough to be pulled up.

I enjoyed the intelligence tests. The word association tests seemed designed to reveal reactions to various situations, such as emergencies, as well as probing our habits and abilities to relate to others where difference of social order, religion or race existed.

The psychiatrist questioned me about my reactions to danger in battle conditions. This led him to ask what arm of the Service I would like if I could not be commissioned into the Artillery.

Tanks, the Armoured Corps, was my choice. My discussion with him seemed cordial and without any awkwardness or argument.

We were informed of the Selection Board results the next morning. I had passed, but to everybody's surprise and to his own bitter disappointment, Walter Brown had not. Those in his syndicate considered him the outstanding person of all they had met. His qualities of leadership and courage were undeniable; his mechanical abilities in gunnery equipment and all motor vehicles exceeded those of the artificers and mechanics. Walter and I talked it over and the only part of the course that he thought could have influenced the Board's decision was his interview with the psychiatrist. He had been asked about his recreational preferences and had spoken enthusiastically of rough-shooting. He was, he had said, fond of taking a shotgun and a few cartridges and walking over a nearby area looking for a rabbit or a pigeon for the pot. The psychiatrist was fanatically opposed to any blood sport and the resultant argument had been acrimonious. It would have been ironic if the psychiatrist's report could have had sufficient weight to fail him, since Walter's ability with a shotgun had carried over to his aiming the Bofors gun so well in action. That surely was an added reason to pass him.

There was little time to do more than speculate, as we had to go our separate ways, he back to the Battery and I to Almaza Barracks, the Artillery depot, to await my posting to the Officer Cadet Training Unit. Referred to hereafter as the O.C.T.U., the site for the Middle East Force was at Acre, a few miles north of Haifa.

On arrival at Almaza, I found that those of us awaiting the posting to the O.C.T.U. were to be given a course in preparation for Acre. We were given the white capbands and sleeves for our epaulettes which gave us the status of officer-cadets. We had our own mess where we were waited on by white-robed and tarbooshed servants. The programme was strenuous; plenty of physical activities and lectures on relevant subjects, a brushing-up of mathematics, and an opportunity to put our uniform into good condition. The Middle East O.C.T.U. was said to be the toughest and best of all such training units and the preparatory course was of great value.

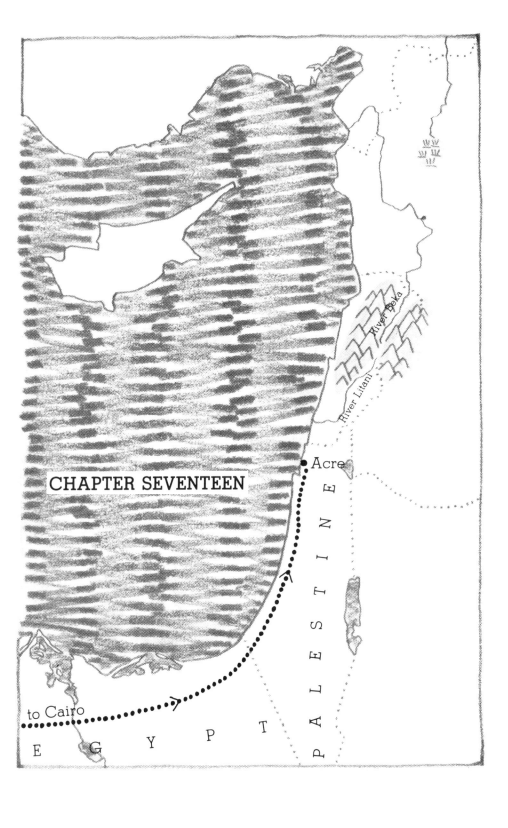

CHAPTER SEVENTEEN

Acre

River Beka

River Litani

PALESTINE

to Cairo

E   G   Y   P   T

CHAPTER 17

OFFICER-CADET TRAINING

Them that's keen, gets on parade previous.
Attributed to an unusually literate sergeant

Our orders arrived for our journey to Acre. We left Cairo in the evening of April 22 1943 and reached Palestine on April 23rd, St. George's Day, after a tiring twelve-hour railway trip on wooden seats. We stopped for breakfast at Lydda, where the chapel dedicated to St. George is located. We were given tea and stew, but best of all we were able to buy juicy Jaffa oranges from Arab boys selling them on the station platform. I recalled as we drew out of Lydda on our way to Acre that it also was Shakespeare's birthday, and I proclaimed a slightly different version of Henry V's speech:

And gentlemen in England now abed
Shall think themselves accursed they were not here
And hold their manhoods cheap whiles any speaks
That rode the train with us on George's day.

The speeches when we arrived at Acre were not much like King Henry's. We were marched around the camp at a brisk 192 steps to the minute, "ep, ite, ep, ite", with frequent stops in front of various buildings while the drill-sergeant told us, "On your right, the Dining Hall," and "On your left, the Adjutant's Quarters. He is Captain A.G.Y. Hubble, M.C."

These names and decorations we were supposed to memorize and we were, indeed, frequently questioned.

"On your right, the Chief Instructor, Major D.S. Fraser, D.S.O., M.C."

He was a tall ginger-moustached Scot who was remembered by cadets for his simple instruction, "If you can't dislodge the Hun any other way, you must go in with the bayonet and winkle him out."

120

Our indoctrination complete, we went to draw our bedding; paillasse, two sheets, three blankets and a mosquito net, the latter a necessity in the hot humid weather of the coast. The bedding served a dual purpose, the usual one to cover us at night and the other - a military innovation - to give us a task measurable for rewards and punishments. Our three blankets had to be folded in exactly the same way. Once in a neat pile, they were enclosed by the two sheets. Finally the mosquito net, which was suspended from a rod above the bed, was folded under blankets and sheets, not obscuring the bedding, but making a tent-like structure in which the exactness and neatness of the whole was instantly visible.

The usual punishments for any "idleness" in a cadet's personal cleanliness or tidiness in bed making was a "wet-shirt." This was an hour's drill taken at the 192 paces a minute in which all our drills were done in the first month of the course. The rigour of the course, exemplified by the punishment, was to instil in us all a high standard of care for ourselves, for our equipment, for our performance in foot drill, physical training and all other activities. It was hoped that this would carry over into the units we served with when we became officers. There has always been adverse criticism of this type of training to inculcate an *esprit de corps,* a suffering together to form a corporate identity. In the British Army, this is very much the creed of the Guards, not only to die with their boots on, but also to make sure that the boots are clean at the time. I think the system can be endured easily if a sense of humour shields it from any excesses of cynicism or concern. It is important as a means to an end, unimportant in itself.

The exponent of the rigours of the drill-square was a New Zealander, a Sergeant Girton. He would lurk behind a drill session and if any cadet failed to finish a movement with his heels together, but tried to bring them together unobtrusively and silently, Sergeant Girton would scream, "Why are you running all over my parade ground?"

Or, if a fly settled on an eye and the victim twitched his eyelid, Girton would shout, "Don't jump up and down in the ranks! Stand still."

We had heard of these stories from the senior cadets and were prepared to look steadily to the front without expression when Girton was around.

121

Friendships are very important. I have previously mentioned Curtis and Day, Stacey and Venables as examples, as well as my own friends, Alan Bellamy and Walter Brown. I had met a Scot at Almaza, waiting as I was for his posting to the O.C.T.U. Like myself, he was a sergeant in a Bofors battery. Ian Balfour was from Edinburgh. He had been wounded in the German invasion of Crete and had been evacuated by hospital-ship. While on the passage to Alexandria the ship had been bombed, with heavy casualties. After recovering in hospital, Ian had been injured when a bren-carrier ran over his feet and he had lost both little toes. He had had to learn to walk again and, after doing so, had been posted to a transit camp in Jerusalem. We agreed to share the experiences of O.C.T.U., to study lecture notes when necessary and to do all the equipment cleaning together to be well prepared in every way possible. This proved useful in minimizing any harassment the system might cause and in keeping our sense of humour unimpaired.

The course at the Middle East O.C.T.U. was strenuous. Reveille was at 5:30 a.m. when a pail of tea - "gun-fire" it was called - was dumped in each of the barrack-rooms. The first parade was at 6:30, in the comparative cool of the morning, and was an hour's drill, preceded by a searching inspection from top to tail, including chin and jowls. ("Stand closer to the razor when you shave, sir.") Any part of clothing or equipment not passing inspection was designated "idle" - "Take that Cadet's name, Sergeant; idle boots!"

Even the roll-ups of shirt-sleeves could be "idle", if not the same width. After the eagle-eyed inspection, the drill began at 192 paces a minute and the comparative cool did not save anybody from a wet-shirt. The laundry service was excellent and gave no excuse for not having immaculate shirts and shorts for all parades.

Very varied activities began after breakfast. Often we were taken to some hilly area where the vegetation consisted of long sharp thorns or spines. There, after discussions, we would be set a problem for which we had to make a plan, perhaps to capture an enemy strong-point. To be successful in our hypothetical attack - in the judgment of the instructor - our plan had to coincide with the "school solution" - that is, the correct answer as agreed upon by the Authorities. These solutions were well-known and were generously passed on by senior and former cadets. The humorists found to their cost that it was not sufficient to quote the Chief Instructor and plan "to go in with the bayonet and winkle the Hun out", even if spoken or written with a slight suggestion of a Scottish burr.

Some field exercises took place after dark. One such was a night compass-march which was held during a moonless period. We were in groups of four and started at five minute intervals. A compass bearing was given and we had to find an instructor on the given bearing, who then checked the group off his list and gave it the next bearing, where another instructor gave the final bearing to bring the groups back to the starting point. The rocky terrain made this a difficult test using only the hand prismatic compass, since it was difficult to maintain the correct course while negotiating the outcrops of rocks. Our group did not use the compass. One member was an extremely tall New Zealander, already famous among other cadets because he never polished his cap badge. By standing his full height, head up, the badge was hidden by the brim of his Boy Scout type hat. No instructor or inspecting officer was tall enough to see over the brim. The "Tall New Zealand Cadet", as he was usually called, was in an Artillery Survey unit and was an expert in astral navigation. On being given the first bearing, he set it on the compass and then glanced up at the dark, clear sky. After a moment's scrutiny, he handed me the compass and said, "Follow me."

This was difficult. The remaining three of us trotted and tripped over rocks in the wake of our navigator as best we could. At the two check-points he asked for the compass, set the bearing, looked up at the sky and then strode off in his seven league boots. When we reached the starting-point again (three of us utterly exhausted), the officer checking the finishers glanced at our start time and then refused to believe we had completed the course. We had, but many groups had not even found the first check-point.

Patrols were also practised at night. I went out, as an observer, with a patrol which was supposed to penetrate enemy-held territory. This small force of ten men was carrying out a reconnaissance to try to assess the strength of the enemy. The area was defended by a similar sized force - what the Army calls a standing patrol - which would operate every night, if it were deemed necessary, to prevent intrusions. A hurricane lamp was placed on a prominent rock to be the objective and the defending force was deployed around it. I stayed with the cadet detailed to command the reconnaissance patrol and heard his orders. He planned to approach the area through orange groves, about three-quarters of a mile long. At the edge of the cultivation he estimated he would be within a few hundred yards of the lamp. He led the patrol very quietly, and, when clear of the orange groves, could see the lamp. Instead of approaching directly, he moved to the right until a hill was between him and his objective. The patrol then scaled the hill and stayed just below the crest while the commander went noiselessly to the lamp and turned it out. He rejoined his men without being discovered and the patrol returned undetected. There was a post-mortem next morning at which I was asked to report. The commander was commended for his excellent effort, as was I for my report on the operation. The defenders had been, in the instructor's opinion, too static, neglecting to cover the steep hillside down which the leader came.

Maps were a frequent topic for lectures. We had practices in map enlarging, in reducing map scales, such as one in a million, to more easily comprehensible forms and in making landscape sketches on the spot to illustrate a reconnaissance report. All this was of great interest to me as my maternal grandfather had spent his working life map making for the Government, mainly in Southern Ireland, and I had inherited a feeling for and an understanding of maps.

We were given demonstrations, often of new weapons. One such was the P.I.A.T. gun, later more commonly known as a bazooka. On this occasion we were drawn up to face the instructor as he explained the working and the use of the gun. When he turned to fire it we were, as we should be, behind the firer. The target was a forty-gallon drum with some oil in it, about fifty yards away. The instructor fired, hitting the drum which burst instantly into flames. At the same time the cadet next to me spun a half-turn and dropped flat on his face, blood streaming from his forehead. A small piece of the casing of the projectile had hit him, stunned him momentarily and cut him sufficiently to cause him to bleed profusely for a few minutes. He recovered in time to have lunch with us.

124

The Saturday morning early parade was an inspection and march past in slow and quick time at which the Commandant took the salute. For this parade we wore white leather belts which had brass buckles worn almost smooth with constant polishing. The belt itself had to be "blanco-ed" and then smoothed with talcum powder. Finally it was wrapped up to be perfect for the parade with the brass undulled. During the long wait while the inspection was being carried out, platoon by platoon, a band of Yugoslavian soldiers played from its repertoire. The inspection finished, the band played suitable martial tunes as we marched past the saluting-base, first in quick time, then in slow time.

The weekends were given over to sport. There was hockey on the parade square, cricket on a matting wicket with a stony outfield, and water polo in the swimming pool. Although we were on the beach, the undertow was so strong that no swimming was permitted in the sea. In my time there, the games were chiefly New Zealand versus the Rest. I played for the Rest in hockey and cricket, both of which we won, but the "Kiwis" won the water polo.

The sports were voluntary, but the physical training was not. There was a period of one sort or another every day. Sometimes we ran over the assault course; at other times, after a muscle-stretching series of exercises, we wrestled; occasionally we had bayonet training, culminating in efforts to knock the straw dummies and their stands over.

Each day, cadets were assigned to duties as cadet-sergeant-majors, cadet-lieutenants and cadet-captains. Their tasks were to take charge of the cadets during the day's parades and activities. The appointees were watched closely by the camp staff for their performance of these duties and for qualities of leadership and power of command. If doubts were raised about a cadet's suitability for commissioned rank, he would be relegated at the end of the course to repeat the second half, or returned to his unit. This happened rarely, since cadets were well screened beforehand and most had proved themselves before being recommended for officer-training. I was disappointed that I had only one such duty, a very minor one as cadet sergeant-major on a quiet day, but it was enlightening to notice those who had several such appointments in quick succession, after doing poorly at first.

My friend Ian Balfour was warned for Company Commander's Orders one morning. This meant he was on charge, though Ian did not know why until he was marched in, and, to his complete surprise, heard our drill-sergeant, who seemed occasionally to be almost human, testify against him. Cadet Balfour's rifle, he said, had rust peeling off it and there were spiders in the barrel! Balfour had the good sense to admit culpability and was awarded three extra drills. We had been warned about these tests and knew it was necessary to find the proceedings neither laughable nor infuriating.

The days fled by. Ian and I continued to go over our lecture notes and to prepare for the next day's activities conscientiously. My next-bed neighbour was Dan, a sergeant in the Irish Guards. He was never in a hurry but always ready; had time to spare to help others; was never tired, rattled or ruffled. I was reminded of the Greek philosopher who had defined a soldier's duty as not merely to fight but to die for his country when some months later I heard to my sorrow that Dan had been killed in action in Italy.

While we were at the O.C.T.U., a Turkish Army delegation visited the camp, part of the diplomatic efforts to bring Turkey into the war on the Allied side. The Germans were making similar efforts on behalf of the Axis forces. Our company was to demonstrate an infantry position in defence. Instead of doing this in a straightforward way, it was decided to do everything incorrectly to add interest. Balfour and I had to dig and man a weapon pit. Since Ian was about six inches taller than I, we dug the pit shallow at Ian's end and deep at mine. When the delegation came round, Ian was protected by the pit only from the knees down while I was unable to see over the parapet. We didn't see a single smile on the Turkish faces and I wondered how they were prevented from throwing their lot in with the Germans.

During the last month I suffered a painful injury when, jumping an obstacle with a deep drop on the assault course, I landed on my heel on a rock and badly bruised the bone. I was hobbling for about two weeks but managed to attend all lectures and most activities.

One day as we were practising the passing-out parade, the drill-sergeant thought we were not working very enthusiastically, so he kept us marching beyond the usual time when drills ended.

A New Zealander, Bob Barret, took exception to this and audibly called the sergeant a bastard, to which epithet, traditionally, drill-sergeants are sensitive.

"Who said that?" he shouted.

Without a moment's hesitation, Bob Genge, A Fijian in the New Zealand Army, stepped out of the ranks and said, "I did."

Now Barrett had been in trouble on two previous occasions and might well have been dismissed from the course and returned to his unit, as Genge knew. There was more to it than that; Bob Genge, who was almost certain to win the Sword of Honour as the best cadet on the course, then and there gave up his chance.

From the Middle East O.C.T.U. we moved to the Light Anti-Aircraft School which was about twelve miles south of Haifa. There were only fifteen cadets on our course and it was a much more relaxed atmosphere that we met here. We occupied two tents set among large shady carob trees. The weather in July is hot and humid, so much so that we dispensed with the tent walls. The gun-park was on the shore about a mile from the camp and there we were drilled on the guns to a high degree of skill. We shot at towed sleeve-targets and also at a forty-gallon drum, pretending it to be a tank, as it was drawn on a long tow along the beach at twenty miles an hour by a jeep.

Ian and I made some interesting trips to Haifa and biblical places - Nazareth, Cana and the Sea of Galilee. Where hitch-hiking failed - and people, Arab and Jew, were most helpful - buses were surprisingly frequent, even in remote parts. We were also able to visit some relatives of Jewish friends of my wife. We were in a bus near Tel Aviv when it became known to the passengers that Ian's family name was Balfour. This went round the bus and ended in a spontaneous round of clapping. Zionists did not forget their great supporter, the one-time British Foreign Secretary, Arthur James Balfour.

When Ian and I were on leave in Jerusalem after being commissioned, our Jewish friends came to take us to a kibbutz. We had, naturally, some idea of the operation of one and were very interested in visiting a communally-run enterprise. All meals were taken in a dining hall; the working mothers had their children cared for; every adult had a job to do. We ate the midday meal in the dining hall. Here songs were sung at every meal and Ian and I were invited to sing. Since we both knew the words, we sang *Loch Lomond*.

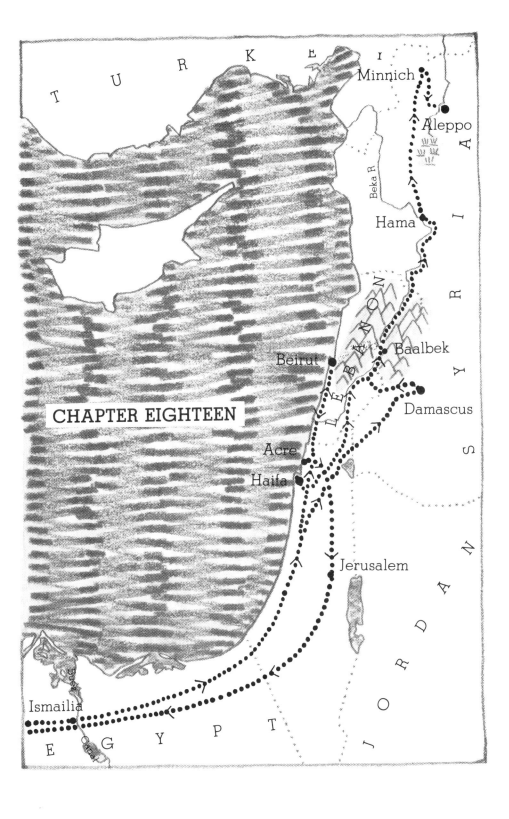

CHAPTER EIGHTEEN

T U R K E Y

Minnich

Aleppo

Beka R

Hama

S Y R I A

L E B A N O N

Beirut

Baalbek

Damascus

Acre

Haifa

Jerusalem

J O R D A N

Ismailia

Suez

E G Y P T

CHAPTER 18

CADETS? NO. OFFICERS? YES!

Self-possession is the backbone of authority.
G.M. Haliburton

It was on a hot humid day in August 1943 when we finally took off our white hatbands and shoulder-tabs and put the single stars of a second lieutenant on our epaulettes. We had a week's leave before reporting to the Royal Artillery Depot in Cairo. Ian had been invited by his former commanding officer to spend the time in Jerusalem and to bring a friend.

With all our kit we begged lifts; first we were taken down the coast road as far as the junction with the road to Jerusalem. It was evening as we approached the city and I understood all I had often said or sung..."City of God how broad and far Outspread thy walls sublime," and, "Jerusalem is built on a hill, that is at unity with itself." Most revealing and stunning was "Jerusalem the Golden," literally true, as the setting sun lit the yellow limestone buildings with an unearthly radiance.

A tent was ready for us; a shower and clean clothes refreshed us after a long hot journey. After dinner we were the guests of the sergeants, Ian's old colleagues. Then, on the flat roof of the administration building, which was lit by a string of lights, we were honoured at a party given by the commanding officer, a major of the Royal Horse Guards. The other guests were presented to us and two interned Italians, a tenor and a soprano, sang operatic duets to piano accompaniments. It was a generous gesture and a most enjoyable send-off to our commissioning.

Ian had, of course, been in Jerusalem long enough before going to O.C.T.U. to know the city well and was an excellent guide. He introduced me to Ben Gurion, who at that time was head of the Jewish Agency and later became Prime Minister. We talked to a scribe who stood at a high desk at the Damascus Gate and wrote letters for the illiterate. We visited General Gordon's tomb, an alternative site for the Holy Sepulchre which we found much more believable than the one in the Church of the Holy Sepulchre. The custodian of the Garden Tomb, as Gordon's is often called, was an English lady who told us that Joseph of Arimathea, who had owned the site, was thought to have traded with Britain and some believed him to have carried the Holy Grail to Britain for safekeeping. Thus it was taken into the Arthurian Legends.

Our leave ended as it had begun, well. A colonel was in the transit camp the night before we had to leave, with his driver and staff car. He generously agreed to take us to Cairo which was his destination. Instead of a tiring train journey of twelve hours, we drove in comfort across the bleak and torrid Sinai Desert, unfriendly compared to the Libyan part of the Sahara. We ate our lunch sandwiches in the shade of an empty water tank. By early evening we had reached Cairo, and Ian and I reported to Almaza Barracks where we would stay until posted to a regiment.

I was given a gun detachment, new to the Bofors gun, to drill at bringing the gun into action, serving it and then taking it out of action. Each of the gun team of six is drilled in each of the six gunners' jobs so that all know them well and can take over any one in an emergency. On the second day of this assignment, I contracted a severe case of "gippy tummy", whose symptoms are stomach pains and diarrhoea. As the nearest latrine to the gun was about four hundred yards away, I had to ask the sergeant to take over while I ran to the latrine and walked back twice or more each hour. It is sometimes difficult to know where "gippy tummy" ends and dysentery begins and I was forced to report sick and spent twenty-four hours in bed until it was certain that I had not the latter disease.

Each evening a lecture was given in the camp to some fifty gunners and junior N.C.O.s who would rather have been anywhere else. My next interim job was to give one such lecture, the subject to be "Causes of the Defeat of France in 1940." A pamphlet gave me some suggested topics to discuss. The Orderly Sergeant marched in my victims, handed them over and vanished. I invited them to sit down and smoke if they wished. Too knowledgeable to use the time-honoured cliche, I did not add, "Those without, go through the motions."

It was disappointing to find that none of my audience had soldiered with the French in 1939/40 either in France or Norway, so there was no opportunity to hear other impressions of French morale. My own impression of the Foreign Legion and the *Chasseurs-Alpins* had convinced me of their fine fighting qualities. The next point suggested in the pamphlet was the great gap in the generation which should have given leadership, caused by the slaughter of the young Frenchmen in the First World War and the consequent fall in the birth rate. This, combined with a lack of will to defend their country, had in a large degree caused the collapse in 1940. At this point a hand shot up and I was glad to see some sign of life.

"What is your question?" I asked.

"Well, sir, about the birth rate, is that why they have all those Yanks and Canadians in England now, so as we won't collapse next time?" That ended the lecture and the audience filed out in a happy buzz of conversation.

A few days later Second-Lieutenants Tilson and Waters were posted to the 16th Light Anti-Aircraft Regiment and were ordered to report to the headquarters at Port Said, travelling by the overnight train from Cairo. Tilson and I felt tired and scruffy when we arrived at Port Said. A truck was waiting for us, and without any opportunity to wash or shave, we were welcomed by the Colonel and consigned to the 83rd Battery, stationed at Kantara on the east side of the Suez Canal. The same truck took us there and we met our battery commander, Major Stebbings, who sent me to "A" Troop and Tilson to "B" Troop. Captain Dick Waring and Lieutenant Alistair McKay were my colleagues in "A" Troop and we had a very pleasant site on the canal bank.

All four regiments to which I had belonged were Territorial units and my present one was, in the quality of its personnel, by far the best. It had been raised some years before the War in a rural area of Kent. In September 1939 it had been below strength and had received reinforcements from all parts of the country which it had assimilated and then moulded to the shape of the well-disciplined cadre.

While the Germans still held Crete, the Canal area was a possible target for bombing; hence the deployment of guns to defend it. These attacks never came and the units detailed for its defence had a boring though safe duty, lightened by the interest of the Canal's constant traffic and cool swims in the evenings.

The railway from Cairo to Haifa and Beirut crosses the Canal at Kantara and the station there has a Customs Control post and a bar. Here, in the evenings, the off-duty officers would gather for drinks. The Customs Control officer was a Captain Bedwell and he and his attractive wife were there most evenings; the night train for Beirut came through at that time and Captain Bedwell supervised the customs examination while the army officers entertained his wife. One memorable night a newly arrived officer, on being introduced, addressed her in Freudian error as Mrs. Bedworthy!

I did not enjoy these simple pleasures for long. As the junior troop officer, I was detailed to attend an Engineers' course for all other arms. It was held a short distance away, outside Ismailia. There was a very mixed bag taking the course - Iraqui, Indian, New Zealand, South African and British officers. We learnt how to build deep pit latrines; to defuse delayed-action bombs; to collect and safely dispose of the butterfly bombs the Germans strewed liberally over our airfields; to blow up houses; to drop trees neatly across roads with a small explosive charge; to fire forty-gallon drums at enemy tanks; to use inflatable boats to cross rivers and to support bridges.

There was a great deal to learn and remember. I was very pleased to finish top of the course and to be recommended as suitable for brigade instructor. Congratulatory letters came to me from brigadier, colonel and battery commander.

A few days after I returned to my unit, the Regiment left the Canal Zone for Amriya, to be fully equipped for a move north into Syria and Lebanon. This occasioned my first big task as an officer and on my own. I had to take drivers from each battery and regimental headquarters to pick up the vehicles needed to make us mobile. On static gun-sites we had a minimum of transportation. The vehicle depot was near Cairo, just short of the Pyramids and Sphinx at Gizeh. I led the convoy with the drivers down the desert road and signed for thirty-nine vehicles. The vehicles were then assigned to their units and each driver took over his own. When all had been claimed we returned, and I, like the Duke of Plaza-Toro, led from the rear to look after any breakdowns. All arrived back safely.

Christmas 1943 found us still in Amriya and we celebrated in the traditional manner with turkey and plum pudding served to the men by the sergeants and officers. I was neatly tripped as I went to deliver two full plates, but, though falling flat on my face, I managed to keep the dinners from spilling or landing in the sand. Raucous cheers greeted this feat as the freely flowing beer took effect.

We set out before the New Year and reached Tulkarm, not far short of Haifa, on the first day. I had a very busy time on a motorcycle making sure all vehicles kept to the route, rather, I thought, like the Good Shepherd.

Next day, the convoy wound through the hills of Galilee and we were eating our lunch by the Sea of Galilee when the brigade commander burst on the scene and blasted Eric, our battery captain, for being behind the scheduled times of the movement orders and consequently holding up everyone else. We were ordered to stay where we were for two hours while the rest of the regiment went through. This meant that we were going to have a very late bedtime, as all realized.

We crossed the Jordan River shortly after resuming our march and continued through the Golan Heights and Kuneitra to the outskirts of Damascus. By this time it was quite dark. We were forbidden to use lights and I was driven off the road when an on-coming truck left me no room. I lost control as I hit some large rocks and as I went down the bike fell on top of me. The handlebars caught me painfully in the ribs. There was no damage to the motorcycle and I caught up the column as it approached our destination for the night, a corrugated iron hutted camp. This was reached by a very steep, muddy, rutted track with a sheer unprotected drop on one side and a rock face on the other. Nineteen times I fell off on the way up; I finally reached the top where Dick Waring picked up the bike for me on my last fall. Next morning we found that a fine, dry, gravelled road was the front approach to the camp and I realized that map reading was not at the top of the Battery's accomplishments!

Our march was to the west until we reached the Beka Valley when our direction was north between the Anti-Lebanon to the

134

east and the Lebanon mountains to the west. We passed the famous Roman ruins at Baalbek where huge dressed columns of rock, meant to be the pillars of another temple but never erected, are said to be the largest single pieces of dressed stone in the world. Our destination was some miles beyond Baalbek, another of the hutted camps which had been built by the French when Syria and Lebanon were their colonies. Now these camps had been given names of famous English soccer teams; whereas last night we had slept in Aston Villa, we now arrived in Huddersfield.

Our route north had taken us along the valley of the Beka River. Hemmed in as it is to the east and west by mountains, it acts as a funnel for the winds which blow strongly during the winter months. I was made aware of this one morning as I stepped out of my hut to go to breakfast. A huge sheet of corrugated iron sailed past and knocked off my hat without damaging me. It continued windborne until out of sight.

Again I was chosen to attend a course, this time at Helwan near Cairo, on German Army equipment and organization. I was driven to Riyak in the Beka Valley where I picked up the narrow-gauge railway which runs from Damascus to Beirut, crossing the Lebanon mountains at about 9,000 feet at the highest point. At Beirut I took the train to Cairo, then the local train to Helwan.

The course was most interesting and my knowledge of the German language was sufficient to enhance my enjoyment of it. There was a great amount of detail to be learnt, particularly in badges of rank, medals, awards, and different piping on uniforms to differentiate the various services. The weapons were studied: small arms, machine-guns, artillery, field and anti-aircraft guns, armoured cars and tanks. The five elements of which all German combat units, whatever their size, were made up - namely, infantry, artillery, armour, engineers and reconnaissance - seemed to me to explain to a great extent the efficiency and flexibility of the German Army. When we were called in to sign our reports at the end of the course, I found that I had tied with another officer for first place and later I had good reason to be pleased that I had done so well.

My return from Helwan by rail ended at Beirut in a minor misfortune. My bedroll, containing camp-bed, pillow and sheets, was not on the train when it arrived in Beirut. The Army R.T.O. (Railway Transport Officer) promised to try to trace it at the stops where the service personnel had left the train and to have it put on the next day's train. Meanwhile I stayed in Beirut to await it. The bedroll did not arrive and the R.T.O. said he would try again, and I remained a second day in Beirut. Again I was unlucky and decided I would have to return to my unit. In the meantime I had found that an Army mail truck went each day to Baalbek with the mail for those units in that area. I rode back in it and, at Baalbek, was able to reach camp on a battery vehicle which was there to collect the mail.

The battery commander, Major Stebbings, was not at all pleased by my late return to the unit. He thought I should have ignored my loss. The battery sergeant-major provided me with a stretcher and three blankets so that I might sleep snugly.

We were soon on the move again. The Battery was ordered to Nahariya, near Haifa, a summer resort area, where there was a firing camp. Here we practised the gun detachments intensively for a week and finished our preparation for a move into the north of Syria, close to the Turkish frontier. Meanwhile British troops dressed as civilians instructed Turkish officers in uniform on British weapons in southwest Turkey while, in the north, German troops dressed as civilians taught Turkish officers in uniform how to operate German guns.

Our role was to be ready to entrain with all our guns and trucks and make as fast a move as possible to Istanbul, if Turkey could be brought into the war on our side. To do this expeditously we had measured all our equipment and were ready to load guns and vehicles into the Turkish rolling-stock. Our site was some twenty miles northwest of Aleppo, within a few yards of the railway. As a secondary role we were protecting an airfield from which reconnaissance planes flew missions over the Eastern Mediterranean and such islands as Crete, Rhodes and Cos, all German held.

The march into northern Syria was pleasant. From Nahariya, we drove east to the Jordan Valley and then followed the river until we entered Lebanon at Metullah. Here we left the Jordan and followed the Litani River in a beautiful valley bright with azaleas on the river banks. To the east the land rose steeply and we could see the Chateau Beaufort, one of the famous Crusader castles on the crest above a sheer cliff. Soon we changed the Litani for the Beka Valley and had reached Baalbek once more. A few miles farther north and we entered Syria. At Homs there were cave dwellings above the road, still inhabited. The houses near Hama, the next town, were shaped like old-fashioned conical bee-hives, and here the plain, in which Aleppo is situated, opened to the four winds.

Our destination was Minnich, a Moslem village where the outgoing battery reported that they had found the inhabitants unfriendly. As soon as we had settled in, Captain Waring called a meeting of officers and sergeants to discuss how we would deal with this difficulty. The consensus was that we should try to establish a better relationship than our predecessors had. Dickie Waring summed it up succinctly: "We'll say 'Sayeeda' to the bastards."

"Sayeeda" is the general Arab greeting.

The weather was very wet and windy. It was impossible to use a vehicle when I visited the gun detachments next day. My route to the first site took me past the village and as three or four men were standing talking, I said my "Sayeeda." Stony stares were the only response, but when I had gone on a few yards, one of the men growled something and a large, yellow, earless dog came at me. I had a leather swagger stick and slashed at the dog each time he attacked. A running fight ensued but luckily the dog was more bark than bite. Eventually, as I neared the gun-site, the sergeant came out with a loaded rifle, and the dog, as though called off, slunk back. A few days later a child fell and cut her knee near one of the guns and the gunners rendered first aid. The child's mother came to the gun with a gift of eggs and from then on everybody was friends.

During our stay I took drivers on training runs up to the Turkish border at Kilis and we gazed across the neutral zone into Turkey. We were also able to spend twenty-four hour leaves in Aleppo. On one such leave I dined in the Baron Hotel, memorable since Lawrence of Arabia stayed there occasionally while writing his thesis on Crusaders' castles. Another favourite haunt was the Blue Cafe, a restaurant and cabaret run by a French couple, who had stayed in Aleppo after Syria had thrown off its colonial status. Here I practised my French on the owners and watched the evening show. Performers were hard to find but once the owners' daughter gave a very polished display of acrobatic dancing and once a team of touring professionals performed the sword dance.

This area was known for its Salukis, the beautiful Arabian hunting dogs fast enough to run down the gazelle. I had long hoped to have one and Madame at the Blue Cafe promised to enquire locally. After a long conversation in French about this, I sat down at a table to watch the cabaret when a civilian with a military haircut came over from the bar, sat by me and asked if I would mind telling him what I was talking about with the owner's wife. He produced his card, identifying him as a member of the S.I.B., the security branch of the Military Police. I had no objection and told him. When I asked him what his interest was in my conversation, he told me that the restaurant was a rendezvous for foreign agents. One such was awaiting a military tribunal in the Citadel, the ancient fortress.

It was said that the German ambassador in Turkey, Von Papen, had told the Turks that, should they declare war on Germany, Istanbul would be reduced to ruins before any of the country's new allies could intervene. This threat insured the neutrality of Turkey, so we were no longer needed in northern Syria. We left to return to Palestine on a typical windy day. The wind blowing strongly against us kept my all-out speed on a powerful motorcycle down to thirty miles an hour. More than that, I ran out of petrol because of the wind. At Hama there was a large riot going on in the square which I skirted nervously; after the Syrians' treatment by the French, all Europeans were likely targets of their animosity. In Syria and Lebanon we took great pains to make it clear who we were -

"Anglais, pas Francais."

PART SEVEN

BSHARRI, 1943

CHAPTER 19

PALESTINE, SYRIA, AND THE CEDARS OF LEBANON

War is the science of destruction.
John C.S. Abbott

After a night in one of the Baalbek camps we returned to Palestine, to a pleasant site near Rehovoth, outside Tel Aviv. No sooner had we unpacked and settled down than we were ordered back to Lebanon for a month's Mountain Warfare Training. Here we were to join other units who had been stationed in Iraq near the head of the Persian Gulf, where the climate was very enervating.

It was a long march for a day's travel and by the time we had passed through Beirut and the long tunnel through solid rock near Byblos, it was dark. We turned inland and started the long climb to Amioun which is about five thousand feet above sea-level. I was somewhat apprehensive riding a motorcycle without lights on mountain roads in pitch blackness. Our destination reached and all accounted for, we were glad to sleep in or around trucks and gun tow-ers.

We awoke next morning among olive trees in a pleasant open area. A short distance from the camp I found wild cyclamen and bee orchis growing in profusion. I had my camp-bed set up under an olive tree, whose lower branches were useful in supporting the mosquito net. We had a quiet day checking and maintaining our guns and vehicles.

In the evening Dick Waring and I walked down the road and met some of the British Infantry regiment from Basra in Iraq. In coarse terms they referred to the area they had left as the world's outlet of the human body's large intestine. They asked what the

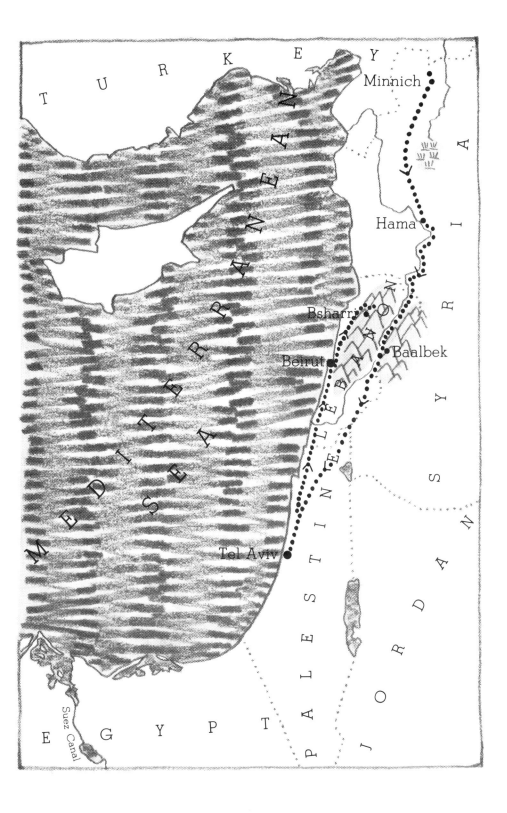

"conner" was like. "Conner" is the Army corruption of the Hindu "Khana", meaning food. Their vocabulary contained many such derived words and seemed Kiplingesque and several generations old. I thought they had been sent more for their health than for training as all seemed far less robust than we and in need of mountain air.

Our training began with daylong exercises for each unit on its own. Towing the guns on the narrow roads where sheer drops of several thousand feet were common was our main concern. Often the hairpin bends were so sharp that our guns had to be unhooked and manhandled, involving the use of wheelchocks, all the men of the gun detachment, and the greatest care in places where it was difficult to keep standing because of the steepness of the road.

The Indian unit of the Brigade was the "Guides", only less prestigious than the "Bengal Lancers." The terrain was a problem for their bren-carriers, which were steered by two handles, each one controlling one track. Whereas on the plains of Iran it didn't matter if the drivers turned left or right, it was literally fatal to turn the wrong way on a mountain road with a sheer drop and a long fall. The Indians, notoriously poor drivers, could and did forget which handle to pull to turn a corner and remain on the road.

We enjoyed the beauty of the mountains, the terraced orchards and vineyards on which the people had to work so hard to build the walls to retain the soil. They were there working when we left camp in the morning and still there when we returned in the evening.

During the day the training plan would send us round and about in the mountains into the valleys and up again. When at last the day's work was over, Captain Waring would often take over my motorbike, hand me his map board, tell me to take his 15 cwt. Dodge truck and lead the troop home. As I had not seen the map since we set out in the morning, I would have to do some hard thinking. Dick never told me where we were, because - I suspect - he didn't know. However, I never failed to bring the troop in, sometimes with a little helpful suggestion from McCreery, the driver.

After our daily training came a three-day scheme which sent us to Bsharri, a village just a hundred feet below the famous

Cedars of Lebanon where there was year-round snow and an Army ski school. It was a miserable wet day when we arrived, and it was difficult to find room to place the guns off the road. At one of the gun-sites the gunners were talking with some of the inhabitants, mostly in sign language. I found that most of the locals understood French and spoke a few words of it. Someone came up and said that her neighbour would like to sing an English song for me. This idea was given general assent and a deputation escorted me to the lady's home where I was seated while she sang *"J'attendrai."* Despite the language, she insisted it was an English song.

Bsharri had an hotel, empty at this time of year, but open for business as the owners and their daughter lived there. The weather was so unpleasant that I suggested to the troop commander that we stay there for the night. He was reluctant, worrying that something might happen, or some "brass-hat" might chance along and find us. Finally, comfort called more loudly than conscience.

The daughter was called "The Brigadier" and wore epaulettes that a brigadier-general had given her. She boasted that she had beaten all comers at table tennis. Perhaps my predecessors had gallantly allowed her to beat them, but I had no such thoughts, winning all the games we played until she went off in a sulk.

After a comfortable night we were up betimes next morning and wound our way down the mountain where the weather was even worse. The exercise was called off and we returned to camp.

The next day the sun shone and I was sent off in the troop jeep to take some documents to Beirut. I therefore drove over the same road by which we had reached Amioun in darkness from Byblos on the coast road. At one point the narrow gravel road forms a causeway between two high points with a sheer drop of about three thousand feet and no guard-rails or protection on either side. On the way that earlier night to Amioun I had ridden my motorcycle, with no lights permitted, across the causeway, unaware of the danger. Years later, a colleague who also had served in this area with a Bofors battery, told me that one of their guns and its tow-er had gone over the edge in the darkness with five fatalities. In both cases there was no good reason to drive in darkness, when a stop at dusk for a night's bivouac would have caused no problems. All too often Army orders were unnecessarily inflexible.

Our next exercise was for the whole Brigade, and I was lent to the battery commander, Major Stebbings, to be his navigator and map reader while he drove his jeep. All the unit commanders, the brigade commander and his staff made up the "O", the Orders Group. The Brigadier would give out his orders and then the commanders would brief their own units. We set out before dawn to the rendezvous on the coast road, the "O" group moving off at 6 a.m.

We drove along the coast road towards Beirut until the column, of which we were the last vehicle, turned inland up a narrow lane which was muddy and contained on both sides by stone walls. A dispatch rider came down the column calling for the commanders to report to the Brigadier for orders. A few minutes later Major Stebbings reappeared, puffing and blowing.

"The Guides are lost," he panted. "They are all trapped in a small farmyard and can't turn round."

He handed me the map board and asked me to tell him just where we were and what had gone wrong. The humour of the situation escaped him at the moment and he was annoyed that I found it so amusing and couldn't stop laughing. We had turned off the coast road to by-pass a small town, but the maps we were using did not show this new road. Whereas we should have turned to the left at the town centre, the by-pass cut the farm lane and therefore the proper turn was the second left. I explained this to Major Stebbings and he dashed back to tell the Brigadier. In turn all the vehicles had to back out of the lane while my commander returned glowing with the congratulations he had received from the Brigadier.

Now that he knew where he was, the Brigadier was able to hold his Orders Group and we left to brief the Battery. I then rejoined my troop. The guns had already been sited and Captain Waring told me to find a suitable spot for the Troop Headquarters. Close to a road and under a precipitous rock-face, I found room for the troop's vehicles and led them into it. No sooner were we comfortably settled than an umpire arrived on the scene and pompously informed us that we were visible to the enemy's ground forces and that they had destroyed us. We were to remain where we were for twenty-four hours. Other than taking rations to gun detachments, we were "hors de combat", and were more than content to have a quiet, restful day. If any blame was received, none reached me, just as no praise came my way for rescuing the Guides when they were lost.

The rest of the exercise was pleasant and the height of the mountains made the heat and humidity much less trying. This was the end of the Mountain Warfare Training and, breaking camp, we returned to Palestine to settle down not far from Lydda and Tel Aviv.

CHAPTER 20

A FAREWELL — AND OFF TO EGYPT

Bury me not, I pray thee, in Egypt.
Genesis XLVII, 20

Only a few days later, my turn for leave came and I left for Alexandria. When last there, after the retreat to Alamein, I had met an old friend. Then I was a sergeant, but now I had been commissioned and was already promoted lieutenant. I wanted him to see the transformation. Basil was working for the Ministry of War Transport and a colleague of his, whom I met, had recently formed an orchestra from Italian prisoners of war and was giving concerts both to the Forces and to the public. During my leave I was able to attend several of the concerts, and wrote critiques of them for *The Egyptian Gazette.*

Alexandria's population did its best to profit from the large influx of troops into the city. Trucks, tires, rifles, and Service paybooks were all saleable commodities. Muggings of personnel were common. One evening I narrowly escaped being a victim. I was with Basil and some of his friends in a favourite restaurant. After dinner we moved to the bar, and feeling unwell, I excused myself and left. Fortunately the hotel where I was staying was close by and I reached the floor where my room was before collapsing. The staff found me and carried me to bed. There was no doubt that I had been given a "Mickey Finn" and that I had been followed, but the nearness of the hotel had saved me from a planned robbery.

The Battery was still near Lydda when I returned from leave. Here we were being bothered with thefts, mainly at night, which were so silently carried out that the guards knew nothing until the loss was discovered. Canvas screens round latrines were a

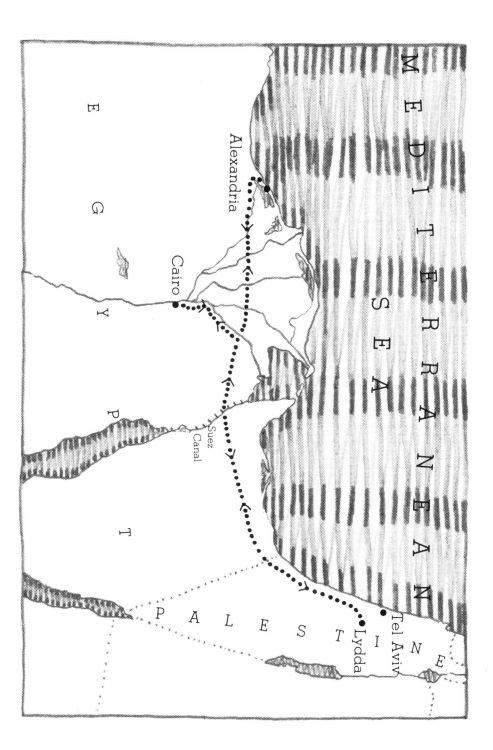

MEDITERRANEAN SEA

EGYPT

Alexandria

Cairo

Suez Canal

PALESTINE

Lydda

Tel Aviv

favourite target. In the end the Royal Engineers were called in to booby-trap them. Some nights later a loud explosion was heard and a young Arab was found, his foot badly injured. He was taken to hospital and we had no more trouble.

Some desultory training was being carried on, though it seemed as if everyone was waiting for something to happen. It had been hoped, with the invasion of Europe unlikely to be put off much longer, that the Regiment might return to England to take part, but instead came the disappointing news that this was not to be.

Instead, the Regiment was to be disbanded as an anti-aircraft unit and retrained for an infantry role. About this time I had noticed that officers were required for intelligence sections in the Middle East where fluent French was a necessary qualification. I thought that I could qualify, and I applied. A week later I was ordered to report to the Middle East Headquarters in Cairo. Eric, the battery captain, was also going to Cairo and I was able to travel with him. We stayed overnight in a transit camp near Tel el Kebir, where I found my old battery also encamped.

The Battery was suffering the same fate as my present unit and was on its way to Cairo to hand over guns, vehicles and stores before beginning conversion to Infantry. Walter Brown had left to join one of the special forces trained to help the Greeks still fighting in the mountains and was doing his paratroop course. The graves of Alan Bellamy and the two gunners, Mellors and Higgins, had been photographed a few days before our retreat and I was given copies of them. Many happenings were recalled, mainly the humour of them, sometimes the sadness.

Next morning, June 6th 1944, the camp was in a state of excitement I had not experienced since September 3rd 1939. The news was good. Landings in Europe were successful on all beaches. Shades of 1914, "It will all be over by Christmas!" We might even be home by then! There were setbacks to come, but that day hearts were lightened and hopes kindled for a home-coming.

My interview at headquarters went well. The major who saw me had my record of service and my letter of application. He explained that there were no longer any openings for which I had applied but he was considering me for a vacancy in a department of Army Headquarters. He noted that I had done well in the course on German army organization and equipment. The job concerned the gathering of intelligence from civilian mail which came to - or was passing through - Cairo, as well as prisoners' of war, internees' and captured mail. The position was for a staff-officer with the rank of captain and would entail living out, with, of course, the appropriate allowances. He said that I might well be the only staff-officer in Cairo with an A-1 physical rating but in view of my record of service since the beginning of the war, he was posting me to fill the vacancy. I was to return to my unit for my belongings and report as soon as possible.

I returned to Palestine on the train and at Lydda I was able to telephone to my battery for transport. While waiting, I happened to notice my long lost bedroll in a corner.

"That's been there for months," the Transport Officer said, pleased to let me take it. The truck came for me and I arrived back at base to be the envy of my colleagues. Many did not look forward to becoming Infantry and opportunities to transfer to other arms of the service were few. I did suggest to Alan Birkett, our troop clerk, that he apply for E.N.S.A., the entertainment organization, which he did successfully, as I learned when we met one day by chance in Cairo.

My last experience in Palestine was embarrassing. The latrines in the camp were of the deep pit type, very well made. On my last visit before leaving for my new posting, I took my wallet from the breast pocket of my bush shirt to check my travel warrant. While looking at it, my wallet slid between my legs and fell into the depths below. It contained my identity card and all my money. The battery sergeant-major heard my sad tale and without laughing suggested I go back and guard against intruders while he organized a rescue operation. A few minutes later he came to the latrine, driving a 3-ton truck. First he lowered an inspection light down through the seat and located the wallet in an unpleasant situation. Next he produced an empty petrol can to which he had secured a long length of wire. This he lowered until it rested on its side right by the wallet. Finally he used a long bamboo pole to push the wallet into the can and triumphantly hauled it to the surface. I gingerly took out the contents of the wallet after which I dropped it back into the pit. After thanking the B.S.M. I went off to scrub my hands, grateful that I had had such expert help.

PART EIGHT
CAIRO, 1944

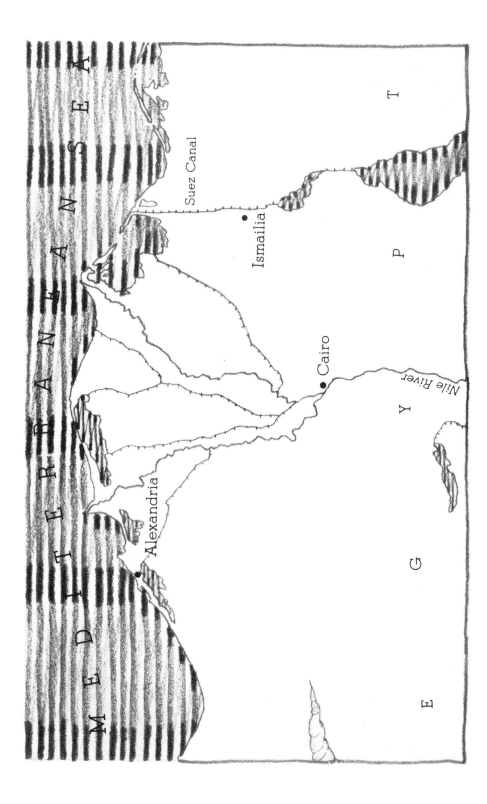

CHAPTER 21

MANNING A DESK

War makes rattling good history, but peace is poor reading.

Thomas Hardy

My first objective on arrival in Cairo was to find somewhere to stay. I found it at the Junior Officers' Club, which, despite its name, was nothing more than a very large boarding house. It was convenient to the office where I would be working, and although each room had two beds, most of the time I had the room to myself. The food was adequate and I took all my meals there.

The office building where I worked was pleasantly situated near the Nile, separated from the banks of the river only by a road. Nearby was the Anglican Cathedral where I occasionally attended Evensong and sat behind General Maitland Wilson, "Jumbo" to his friends.

The purpose of the organization I had been posted to was to collect information ("intelligence" in the Army's jargon) from mail sent to and from addresses who were listed as security risks, including civilian internees and prisoners of war. Sometimes the Navy would intercept small ships bringing supplies to German garrisons from Greek islands in the Aegean Sea and would send bags of mail meant for the garrison for us to examine. Army orders, newspapers, periodicals and letters for the men from friends and families were a valuable source of intelligence, especially of the civilian morale in Germany, though the writers usually minimized anything that might worry husbands or sons.

The documents deemed of interest were, if not in that language, translated into French. This was necessitated by the fact that it was not possible to hire enough competent translators whose first language was English to translate from other languages.

The others in the department in which I was to work were all professors from the University - John Whitehead, Classics; David Abercrombie, son of Lascelles Abercrombie the poet, Economics; John Spears, Mediaeval English; and Walt Taylor, who was compiling an etymology of James Joyce's works. He was responsible for the cables which came through Cairo.

Our task was to direct information gleaned from letters to the department concerned. Sometimes the information had to be inferred, perhaps from a crude code. In letters from German-occupied countries people were mentioned as having various "complaints", which meant they had been arrested or had joined a resistance organization. Trust in the sanctity of the mails was shown when the keys to these simple codes were sent openly by post. To me, as the military expert, fell the responsibility of examining the prisoners' of war mail. Each month I wrote a report on the prisoners' and internees' mail from Germany, chiefly to assess the morale of the civilians and to summarize other main topics. At the time I arrived in Cairo many correspondents were writing of the new weapons, the flying bombs and rockets with which Hitler was promising to force England to sue for peace - according to Goebbel's propaganda, now shriller than ever as hope of victory faded.

Simi is a small island of the Dodecanese archipelago, close to the Turkish mainland and near the northern coast of Rhodes. There was a German garrison on Simi and the supplies of mail, official and personal, were captured when the Greek caique carrying them was intercepted by the Royal Navy. The mail came to me and I examined first the orders sent to the island garrison's commanding officer. A quick glance convinced me that I was wasting my time. The first paragraph of the orders read, "Blankets are not to be used as tablecloths, cushions or curtains..." The second directed the commanders to ensure that those leaving the garrison for evening leave were inspected and warned to behave correctly. All armies' orders follow similar patterns.

The personal mail was very different. One man was written to by mother, sister, aunts and an uncle, a total of twenty-eight letters from which I was able to build up a very complete biography of the man. His family had a small farm and their news revolved around it and the difficulties the war had caused them. Hitler received no mention, but "Wolf" the dog proved newsworthy, and so did the pigs! I was able to name many of his relatives. The finished biography was printed, as an example of the necessity for those who examined the letters to realize the importance of small details. A copy was sent to the department which carried out interrogations of prisoners, and, by coincidence, the entire garrison of Simi was captured when raided by commandos. A report was sent to me describing the utter amazement of the man when he found out that the Allied Armies even knew the name of his dog!

There were others staying at the Junior Officers' Club, who, like me, were not transient. We came to know each other and one inquired if I would be interested in sharing an apartment. We discussed the financial implications and concluded that four of us sharing a two-bedroom flat could manage on our living allowance with two servants to cook and clean for us. Two others were found willing to share.

The apartment was on Midan Tewfik, a circle at the head of one of Cairo's main streets in the city centre. With it came two Sudanese servants: the elder, the cook; the other, the *suffragi* - waiter and cleaner. Most of our allowance went to pay for the rent, the servants and all meals. The bar was kept stocked by one of us who had connections with a brewery and we paid cash for our drinks. I collected the money and paid the rent, servants and food bills. It was a much happier way of life than residence in the Officers' Club and we all enjoyed it.

Walter Brown was one of the first whom I entertained in the apartment. We had met by chance in the street when he was waiting in Cairo to be flown into Greece to aid the Greeks in their guerilla war against the Germans. He had just finished his parachute course in which his last jump, at night, had resulted in a scraped face, the scars of which were still visible. Walter did not very much like orthodox regimental soldiering, and was happy to be going from it to fight in conditions where his ingenuity and aggressive attitude would be far more useful. The next time I saw him, he had very interesting stories of ambushes on mountain roads and of a long hazardous journey he had to make to the island of Ithaca, home of Ulysses, to rescue an R.A.F. pilot.

Whether it was due to the ascetic life that I was leading I do not know, but on three occasions during my stay in Cairo I had very strong thought-transference or E.S.P. experiences. I was going back to the apartment for lunch one very hot day, walking as usual on the shady side of the road, when I began to have a most uncomfortable feeling as of impending calamity. I felt a strong, almost irresistible urge to cross the road, against my usual habit, to the sunny side. The sensation of an imminent occurrence became stronger until I came to the Gaumont Theatre, the only air-conditioned one in Cairo and a popular troop rendezvous. Then my hand was suddenly grasped and there was Harold Stacey, the strong pillar of my gun detachment in the desert fighting of 1942.

"I have been standing here for an hour," he said, "willing you to come past."

He had chosen the best possible place to be, he explained. As soon as he spoke, my feeling of doom vanished. He was now Sergeant Stacey, on leave and, knowing I was in Cairo, anxious to look me up. We spent the afternoon reminiscing until I had to go back to my work and he to his unit.

My second experience was similar in many ways, but more remarkable in the manner I was led to the thought emanations that were calling me. I had dined in the flat and the others had gone out. Instead of settling down to a book as I usually would, I was restless for some while before I realized why. The urge to go out - somewhere - became stronger. Once outdoors I began walking without conscious thought of where I was going. After a few minutes I walked up the steps and into Shepherd's Hotel. It took me some time in the large crowded bar to make sure there was no one there I knew. I went to the reception desk and, without thinking, asked for Major Stebbing's room number. Yes, he was registered in the hotel. The clerk phoned his room, but there was no reply; perhaps he was in the dining room. I knew at once that he was, and when I appeared at his table where he was dining alone, Major Stebbings said almost exactly what Harold Stacey had. Because of a physical disability he had been rejected for the Infantry when the Battery was converted, and was hoping I might have a suggestion for him. I had, since a major in my department was going home and I was able to tell Major Stebbings where to apply for the vacancy. I had had no knowledge that Major Stebbings was in Cairo that evening.

The third incident was less striking but very similar. I had visited the Polish Club with a friend and had arranged to meet him there before going to a cinema. When I went to the club to pick him up the lounge was empty, and I knew at once, from the "extrasensory" feeling that I had now come to recognize, that the was not in the building. Before I had decided what to do, the steward came in and handed me a note in which my friend explained that he had to stay on duty to replace a sick colleague.

In a different vein, we arranged to meet at the Cairo Y.M.C.A. My Polish friend did not understand and was puzzled.

"Pourquoi M.C.A.?" he asked.

Finally I wrote the letters down. Enlightment shone from his face.

"YIMKA! YIMKA!" he shouted.

Life in Cairo was very pleasant. My office hours were 8:30 a.m. to 1 p.m. and 5 p.m. to 9 p.m. After luncheon I usually rested, and about four o'clock walked slowly to Groppi's, where I enjoyed tea and the famous pastries over the English newspaper. After dinner, which we ate a little after nine o'clock, I sometimes went to the nearby "Bar Russe." Despite its name, French was the preferred language - good practice for me! I was talking there one night to some South Africans when five or six Gurkhas came in. Are they allowed in here? Yes, anybody, everybody. The South Africans downed their drinks. "Can't stay here if blacks come in," they said, and left.

Neither I nor any British soldier ever thought of Gurkhas as black, only as comrades and friends with a mischievous sense of humour.

Cairo was an interesting place with diversions for all tastes. I enjoyed the open-air cinemas, where I saw many French films (with Arabic subtitles) - such classics as *"Le Carnet de Bal," "Les Perles de la Couronne,"* the Pagnol films of the Marseilles waterfront and many others. I saw the Tutankhamun display. The Israeli Orchestra gave concerts - once a Mozart and Bach week. The famous Gezirah Sporting Club threw open its facilities to British officers and there was much athletic activity; cricket, soccer, rugby and track and field meets.

Amidst all these pleasures there was a strong anti-British feeling fostered by the King of Egypt. He had many Italian friends who were kept out of internee camps by his protection. In the hot August days, when the Nile was at its highest level and the consequent humidity most oppressive, the Egyptian populace could be persuaded to demonstrate and even riot. On these occasions we were ordered to wear revolvers and to escort the female staff to their homes. During one such riot a huge stone-throwing mob gathered outside the British Embassy and dragged some Europeans out of their taxis, though without injuring them. At that moment, the relief Embassy Military Guard came from the barracks, three men and a corporal. The crowd politely opened a passage for the guard and stopped rioting until the guard had marched into the Embassy grounds!

We hoped to celebrate Christmas with some semblance of tradition and our cook assured me that he could produce a turkey for dinner. It fell out that I was on duty on Christmas morning and had to go to the office until one o'clock. After breakfast, therefore, I went to the kitchen to make sure all was in order. There, behind a door, gobbling in a bad-tempered manner, was a turkey, very much alive. Before I could say anything, the cook asked me to unlock the cabinet where we kept the spirits and to let him have a double brandy.

"Why do you want that?" I asked.

"Not for me, *Effendi,* for Turkey, before I kill him. Very good, very tender, then."

I complied and some five hours later we ate an excellent turkey dinner.

PART NINE
LONDON - PARIS - BONN, 1945

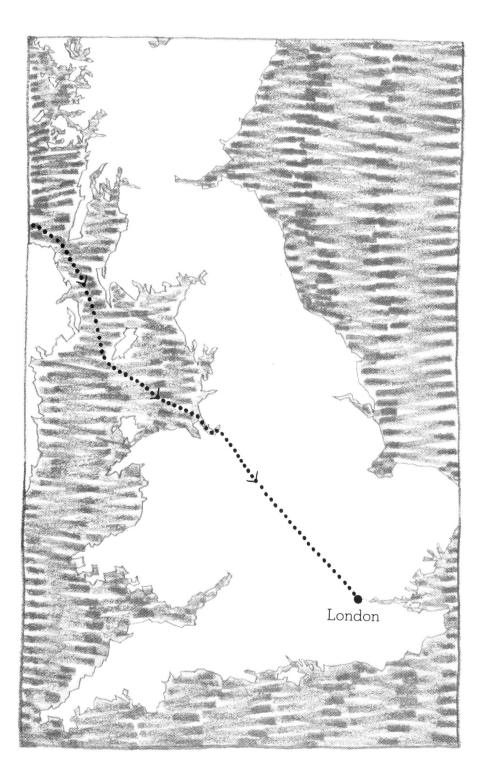

London

CHAPTER 22

INTERLUDE - AT HOME!

Peace hath her victories, no less renowned than war.

John Milton

"Python" became an important word in the New Year, 1945. It was obvious that the war was won and "Python" was the Army scheme to send home all those who had had five years or more service abroad. Since the authorities had allowed me less than six months in the U.K. after I had returned from Gibraltar - only five days less - this did not constitute a break in my overseas service, which was reckoned from April 1940 when I had embarked for Norway. This meant I would be eligible in April 1945 for repatriation. However, the five-year veterans were all cleared before then, and those with four years and eleven months overseas service - including me - were told to be ready on short notice.

About this time a Major Smith in our organization went home, and I was asked to forego my "Python" posting and replace him. I agreed to this, provided I was given his rank. My regiment, the Royal Artillery, would not agree and I therefore left for Alexandria and took passage on the *Duchess of Richmond,* for Liverpool and home.

Before my month's leave was over, the war in Europe was near its end. I was in England in time to hear and see one of the last flying bombs as it buzzed towards London, and to be near enough to hear the devastating explosions of two rockets. These were frightening weapons to a frontline soldier, arriving and exploding as they did before the noise of their approach could give warning.

I returned to my regimental depot, the Royal Artillery Barracks at Woolwich, at the end of my leave in April, but was sent to the Intelligence Corps, which had its headquarters in a magnificent country house, Wentworth Woodhouse, near Rotherham in Yorkshire. All I was required to do there was to return each night in case I was posted to a unit.

The evening meal at Wentworth Woodhouse retained a certain ceremonial not usually met in wartime. About fifteen minutes before dinner was served, all those "dining-in" that night gathered in the anteroom. Precisely at the time for the meal, the permanent staff, led by the commandant, entered the anteroom, whereupon the dining room door was opened and we followed the commandant and his staff to seats at the long table.

One day I was required to appear before the camp commandant, the Earl of Northesk. He had been a Cresta Run winner on the one-man luge-toboggan in the 1920s. There was difficulty, it seemed, in finding a posting for me as my records did not specify my work in Cairo. I explained what I had been doing there and that a colleague who had preceded me in returning from Cairo had been posted to similar duties in a 2nd Army Intelligence Unit. This solved the matter and I was sent first to a testing department of the Intelligence Corps. There I passed as an interpreter for French and was posted to the 2nd Army Rear Headquarters, part of which was in a store building in Oxford Circus.

My first job was to give a short course on Army procedures to civilians who were being commissioned directly in Allied Military Government positions in captured enemy territory. I taught them how and when to salute, to conduct summaries of evidence, courts of inquiry and courts-martial as set forth in King's Regulations and Military Law. My students had to know how to use their side arms, .38 calibre revolvers, and I took them through the necessary instruction and target practice.

162

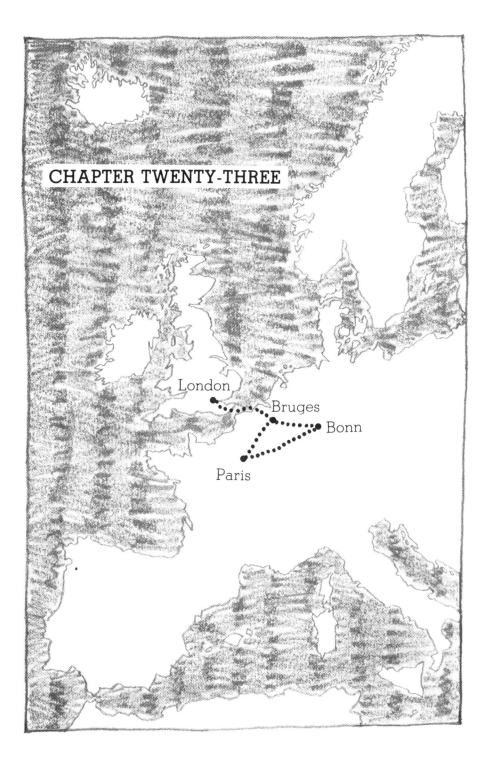

London

Bruges

Bonn

Paris

CHAPTER 23

ON ACTIVE SERVICE - IN A CHAIR

And when the war is done and youth stone dead,
I'll toddle safely home and die in bed.
                                    Siegfried Sassoon

Peace came to Europe and was celebrated May 8th. Our office in London closed and we were transferred to Bruges. We crossed the Channel on a particularly rough night in a converted landing-craft.

In Bruges we were quartered in a rather seedy hotel whose previous guests had been the Gestapo. Our offices were in a large store whose front entrance gave on one of the main streets not far from the town square and the famous Belfry. We used a small door set in a high brick wall in an alley at the rear. The front door was always locked. Here we trained Belgians who had the necessary qualifications in languages to act as translators of mail. They also had to be able to judge whether the contents were useful to the authorities for security or scientific information.

The trainees were billeted in houses near our offices and to help us we also had a small detachment of the Belgian Army under the command of Major Bauwens. A legendary Resistance leader, he was our liaison officer to facilitate arrangements for our recruiting team. Much of this was done in such centres as Ghent and Brussels, and later we went to Antwerp and Tilburg (Holland).

Mail both to and from the German forces had been stranded at the end of the war in Europe. This provided our students with plenty of practice and interesting information from the younger soldiers, many of whom wrote home to tell their wives or mothers that they intended to become "werewolves", fading into the woods to fight as guerillas. From the families, at least before Hitler's death, hope in the "new weapons" was expressed in

164

many letters. Often they would enclose a few tightly wrapped coins in the envelope to their sons or husbands.

I had not been long in Bruges when a forty-eight hour leave in Paris was offered. No one wanted it but me, and off I went by truck to Brussels, thence to Paris on an overnight train. The leave hotel was in the Rue St. Honore. The Louvre and the Folies Bergeres offered widely different cultural experiences, and I was able to find a business associate of pre-war days, Jacques Meisonnier. He had a public relations post in an organization called *"La Rayonnement Francaise"*, which was trying to mend France's war-damaged image.

On the return journey to Brussels, again by the overnight train, I was joined in my compartment by a young American, a driver for a Quaker ambulance unit. Just before the train pulled out, a voluble Frenchman came in and complained in French - he spoke no English - about his leave, only twenty-four hours after six months away from his wife, and, of that twenty-four hours, more than twelve were spent in travelling and, in effect, he did not spend even one night with his beautiful wife after six months' separation because of the incredible train service which ran only at night, unbelievable, is it not?

I tried to keep the young American abreast of the Frenchman's tale of woe. He had a little French of the high school variety, but not enough to understand the realities of the situation. Meanwhile the narrative continued: only eight hours at home after a complete separation - an interminable six months far from his wife, what cruelty, so short a leave...

The American could stand it no longer. He mustered up most of his French to take his part in the conversation. He asked, *"Comment avez-vous passé le temps avec votre femme?"*

The Frenchman's eyes bulged; his face registered disbelief. He was temporarily rendered speechless.

"Did I say something to offend him?"

"No," I replied, "but don't expect an answer."

It was very hot in the train and the Frenchman had brought a large bottle of red wine diluted with some mineral water which he generously shared with us. I slept for the rest of the night and when I awoke at Brussels I was alone.

Our role as part of the 2nd Army Intelligence was primarily to organize and train a staff capable of censoring German postal and telegraphic services. As a result of the training programme, a considerable amount of information was passed on to the relevant departments as well. In August 1945 it was apparent that the time had come to move into Germany to establish the necessary censorship. For this, Major Panton, an A.M.G. officer, and I were ordered to Bonn to choose a location, which could quickly be made ready to house the organization, from a number of German Army barracks. We drove to Bonn and found the officer who was to brief us. He could have doubled as Groucho Marx. He wanted to know our choice of barracks, and requested a detailed plan and time-table to cover the housing of several hundred civilian employees and army personnel, British and Belgian, who supplied the services: security, transport and catering. Our plan had to include finding, with the barracks, nearby houses for the civilians in an area which could be enclosed with the barracks to provide an enclave secured by fences and guards.

It was an extremely hot day. Panton and I made our choice of barracks and then decided on two adjacent streets for lodgings. We drew up a schedule of the work necessary to repair the barracks and to have the present owners of the houses evicted. The Mayor of Bonn would have this unpleasant task and would also try to find accommodation for those made homeless. By late afternoon we had finished, and we sought to present our plan to the officer responsible for preparing the chosen premises who had requested it. We found him in the swimming pool, located in the garden of the house which contained his office. He cheerfully told us, with a Groucho-like smile, how pleasant it was to be able to keep cool despite the heat wave. We agreed it was a better way to spend a hot day than inspecting barracks.

I returned to Bruges in a 15 cwt. truck which had brought office equipment for the advance party. Private Walker was the driver, and a Belgian soldier was comfortably installed on bedrolls in the canvas-hooded back. It was a wet day and, after going through Hasselt on the Brussels road, there were many signs in English warning that the road was very, very slippery when wet. As Walker, after overtaking a large Air Force truck, seemed to be cutting in rather sharply, I said "Don't", but realized after the one word of warning that we were skidding. We spun round to the other side of the road where the trams ran on railway lines. Still spinning we hit the lines broadside on and overturned beyond them. Walker and the Belgian were flung out and I found myself wedged against the steering column, head down. Walker called out to me and I said I was all right. I struggled and after a short while emerged. Neither of the other two was visible, having already been carried into a cafe opposite. Walker had a broken shoulder and the Belgian a back injury, and both were soon in an ambulance and off to hospital. My damage was chiefly to my uniform. My leather capstrap had burst behind the badge - how I don't know - and while extricating myself I had been aware of something dripping copiously on to me. I had worried about fire, but nothing happened. The truck was completely levelled down to the chassis. It was an instant "write-off" and I was able to pick up a replacement the next day. This delayed me and I was billeted in a very pleasant home overnight. When I awoke next morning, the accident had caught up with me. Movement was very difficult and painful; even a very hot bath did little to alleviate the extensive bruising. Some two weeks later, while I was seeing off a contingent of trainees for Bonn, the back of my trench coat suddenly fell in ribbons, the result of the battery acid spilled on it!

Back in Bruges it fell to my lot to send off the last of the civilians to Bonn by train and to close down the office. There were still a few more recruits arriving and one of these turned out to be a very important one. All applicants were subjected to three interviews, much the same in content but each in a different language. Before we accepted them, the Belgian Secret Police were given the sheets for them to investigate the applicants. In the last batch they found a man who was high up on their list of war criminals. He had gone to Germany initially as forced labour, but had been responsible for the deaths of Belgian workers after being given special powers by the Germans. The police had watched in vain the apartment in Brussels which he had given as his address. We decided to try to trap him by writing an acceptance to that address, asking him to report to Bruges on a morning train where we would meet him. I arranged for two Belgian soldiers to arrest him when the truck brought him from the station.

On the evening before he was due, I was in the office with a Belgian soldier when the suspect walked in, having come on an afternoon train. When I had sat him down to fill in some forms relating to billeting and employment rules, I excused myself to tell the very frightened young Belgian - who had left the room before me - to go quickly and bring the police. It was a long fifteen minutes before they arrived, but their entrance was dramatic. The man turned as he heard them enter the office. The moment he saw them his face turned green, from chin up to forehead. He sagged in the chair and was unable to stand unaided as the police took him away. In the small suitcase he had brought with him was the regulation German issue automatic pistol. He was executed some six weeks later. I politely refused an invitation to the execution.

The dispatch by rail of the remaining civilians caused me some trouble. Rolling-stock was in short supply and a promised departure date had to be postponed. Since the unit headquarters staff, now at Bonn, was expecting the train's arrival, I had great difficulty in sending a message to advise them of the change. Our only means of communication was the telephone controlled by the Army Signal Corps. A system of priorities ruled these calls and waits of twenty-four hours were common. After some fruitless efforts, I decided that for the purpose of the call I would have to make myself at least the commanding officer of my unit and would thus claim top priority, number one. The signaller who took my request asked me to hold on while he asked the brigadier-in-charge to talk to me. A few minutes later he came on the line.

"Good afternoon, sir, I presume I am speaking to Field Marshal Montgomery, am I not?"

I was forced to say he wasn't.

"To whom, then, *am* I speaking?"

I had to confess that he was speaking to Captain Waters. He then gave me a long speech on the serious nature of such an impersonation. Finally I was able, very apologetically, to explain my problem. He was sternly sympathetic and ordered me to stay by the phone till the call was put through. There was a delay of some hours but I was able to warn the unit of the postponed departure.

Bruges was now finished with. When I reached Bonn there was no permanent accommodation for the officers, so I stayed in the Officers' Transit Hotel. It was pleasant and, since we were all able to speak German, we were on good terms with the hotel staff and found that there was a reasonable cellar of Rhine wines. The waiter produced the wine for us each evening at a price we appreciated. He had served in the German Army and, when the war ended, did not trouble to wait for any official discharge but made straight for the family home. Before he arrived, however, the occupying power had found and liberated his cache of liquor. Deadly serious, the waiter said, "Next time, *we* will win the war and do the looting."

The restoration of services in German cities and the cleaning of the rubble was a monumental task, but the industry of the people was never more evident. Cologne rose from its ashes within weeks. In Bonn the barracks we had chosen for our organization were being repaired and we managed to have some German soldiers, who were waiting discharge, to help with the task. They were so poorly fed that many fainted while working and, until we were able to give them a midday meal, little was done.

In the roof of the barracks there were many skylight windows which had been shattered. I went up one day to see how much was being accomplished here. One very old man was working alone. I watched him as he placed a sheet of glass over a skylight, took out his glass-cutter, and - without a ruler, by eye alone - made four cuts. He tapped the glass gently in the middle. The pane fell smoothly into place, an exact fit.

At the transit hotel our food was Army rations, always sufficient but without variety. Occasionally we dined out at the Bishop's Palace at Bad Godesberg. Here a restaurant was opened for officers and luncheons and dinners were served each day. There were no choices, just two set menus. Wines were offered and a reasonable selection was available. To help the digestion, a string quartet of very good German musicians played morning and evening.

The palace contained a magnificent salon with huge standard chandeliers, a stage which the musicians used and a grand piano. It was in this room one Sunday morning, when a large gathering was chatting over a pre-lunch drink, that an Air Force officer sat down at the grand piano and began to play jazz, *fortissimo*. The noise offended most of the company and a smaller

169

number were scandalized by the choice of music, considering the beauty of the historic building and the fact that it was Sunday in a Bishop's Palace. Eventually a grey-haired Army officer walked purposefully to the piano, rapped on it for silence and said, heard by all in the room, "Are you aware, sir, that it was in this very room that Beethoven first met Haydn?"

In 1918, after the armistice of November 11th, my father's regiment had marched to Bonn as part of the army of occupation. While in Bonn my father had contracted rheumatic fever. He was billeted with a German family who had been very kind to him, especially during his illness. He had corresponded with them for many years after his return to England. As soon as I knew that I was going to Bonn, I had written to my mother for the family's address. Unfortunately she was unable to find it among my father's papers. I wondered whether they were among those evicted from the streets we had planned to use to house our civilian and military personnel.

Demobilisation was well under way now, and since I had been serving for over six years and was in my thirties, it could not be long before my discharge. Before that happened I was asked to defer it or to become a regular soldier. This I was loth to do, not only because I would lose my rank, but because peacetime service did not attract me.

My orders ending my military service sent me first to Tournai by train, where a school had been made into a transit camp for an overnight stay. Here I ran into an old school friend, Geoffrey Brown, whom I had not seen since he was in training as a doctor at Guy's Hospital. He too had spent much of his service in Africa. We exchanged tall stories of our experiences, but next morning were on different drafts.

From Ostend I sailed on calm seas and fair winds to Dover, and, in the afternoon, chose my civilian suit, shoes, shirt, tie and hat.

I had survived six years and three months of war almost unscathed.

QUO FAS ET GLORIA DUCUNT UBIQUE.

"Where duty and glory leads - everywhere."
Motto Royal Artillery

The Royal Artillery has no battle honours. Hence "Ubique" -
"Everywhere" - on the badge. The regiment carries no colours -
its *guns* are its colours.

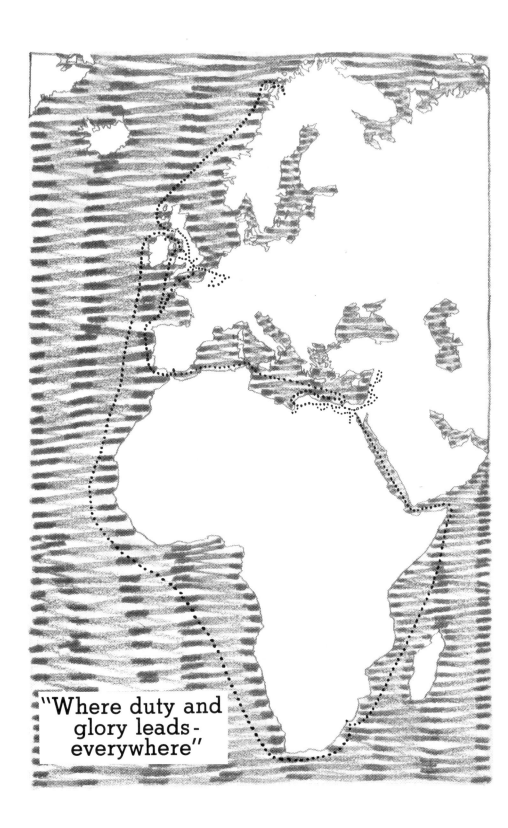

"Where duty and glory leads - everywhere"

After demobilization in October, 1945, **Stuart Waters** taught in Norfolk, England, until 1954. He emigrated to Canada and joined the teaching staff of Hillfield-Strathallan College, an independent school in Hamilton, Ontario. At the time of his retirement in 1977 he was working on *One Man's War,* his first book. Mr. Waters, his wife Helen and daughter Elizabeth currently live in Hamilton. Son Jonathan is a partner in a computer firm in the United States and son Christopher is an officer serving with Lord Strathcona's Horse.